Karen Stiller has written exquisitely and powerfully about life; it just so happens that her window on the world is that of a clergy spouse. Here is a memoir about the joys and sorrows, the pathos and the delights of giving and receiving, of knowing and being known and walking the Christian journey with grace and integrity. Karen's honesty will both surprise and encourage you. You will be refreshed by her lack of platitude, cliché, and religious jargon.

GORDON T. SMITH, PhD, professor of systematic and spiritual theology and president, Ambrose University, Calgary, Alberta

Pastors' wives are people too! Mark and I laughed, sighed, and sometimes cringed as we, through Karen's vivid stories, relived many of our own experiences in pastoral ministry. Who wants a pastoral couple at their Grey Cup party? And who wants you tagging along on their vacation? Karen's been there, done that. Yet she also beautifully evokes the sacred privilege of pastoral work, of the times we get to walk with others in their most difficult or joyous seasons. "Church hurts. Church heals." This is the wisdom at the heart of this book.

CHERYL BUCHANAN, spiritual director and speaker

MARK BUCHANAN, author, speaker, professor at Ambrose Seminary, and former pastor

We love Karen's bold and beautiful memoir! Transparent and vulnerable, funny and wise, uplifting and moving, it is a joy to read. If you're a minister's wife or a minister, you will see yourself in the pages of this book. If not, you'll get a rare and privileged look at what life is really like *inside* the fishbowl.

KEN SHIGEMATSU, senior pastor of Tenth Church, Vancouver, British Columbia, and author of *God in My Everything*

SAKIKO SHIGEMATSU, minister's wife and translator of *God in My Everything* (Japanese edition)

In *The Minister's Wife*, Karen Stiller skillfully and wholeheartedly draws readers into her day-to-day experiences, allowing us to see and feel the joys and struggles of being a minister's wife, pointing us always to trust God to lead and carry us.

ALLISON BEACH, wife of the archbishop of the Anglican Church in North America

Ministry can be described as both brutal and beautiful—"brutiful." Karen Stiller knows. With openness, honesty, and delightful reflection, Karen writes her story of living out her calling as a minister's wife. It's a story that will be understood by all who have fallen in love, obeyed that divine tug toward ministry, and entered into an adventure that was downright challenging, yet amazingly transforming. As a former minister's wife, I recalled my own journey while reading with captured attention. It's strange how reading through Karen's journey helped me make more sense of mine. Well-written and captivating, *The Minister's Wife* is hard to put down. Karen answers many questions that will help others see ministry as more beautiful than brutal.

MARGARET GIBB, founder and executive director of Women Together, Canada

Karen has perfectly captured the unique challenges facing clergy spouses. I commend her bravery for sharing her personal journey. This book is a tonic for those of us who feel inadequate and insecure in this role. It will also provide insight to church members who may not understand the expectations and pressures felt by pastoral partners. Karen's self-deprecating and humorous style makes this a very enjoyable read. I could hear her laughter throughout the book!

CATHY PARKER, clergy spouse

Honest. Realistic. Heartwarming and encouraging. You will laugh and cry and identify with Karen Stiller in her walk with Jesus as the minister's wife.

CHARLEEN ANDERSON, clergy spouse

In this winsome memoir, Karen Stiller hospitably welcomes us into her life as a minister's wife, courageously revealing struggles and challenges all of us will recognize, even if we don't live in similar fishbowls of scrutiny. With humor and transparency, Karen names aloud the kinds of thoughts, doubts, and failures we're often reluctant to confess, and she gently reminds us that we share this ordinary and rare, messy and grace-filled life together. What a gift.

SHARON GARLOUGH BROWN, author of the Sensible Shoes and Shades of Light series

The Minister's Wife

* * *

a memoir of faith
doubt
friendship
loneliness
forgiveness
and more

the Minister's Wife

Karen Stiller

TYNDALE
MOMENTUM®

The Tyndale nonfiction imprint

Visit Tyndale online at tyndale.com.

Visit Tyndale Momentum online at tyndalemomentum.com.

TYNDALE, Tyndale's quill logo, *Tyndale Momentum*, and the Tyndale Momentum logo are registered trademarks of Tyndale House Publishers. Tyndale Momentum is the nonfiction imprint of Tyndale House Publishers, Carol Stream, Illinois.

The Minister's Wife: A Memoir of Faith, Doubt, Friendship, Loneliness, Forgiveness, and More

Designed by Dean H. Renninger

Edited by Bonne Steffen

Published in association with the literary agency of Westwood Creative Artists Ltd., 386 Huron St., Toronto, ON M5S 2G6.

For information about special discounts for bulk purchases, please contact Tyndale House Publishers at csresponse@tyndale.com, or call 1-800-323-9400.

Library of Congress Cataloging-in-Publication Data

Names: Stiller, Karen, author.
Title: The minister's wife : a memoir of faith, doubt, friendship, loneliness, forgiveness, and more / Karen Stiller.
Description: Carol Stream : Tyndale House Publishers, [2020] | Includes bibliographical references.
Identifiers: LCCN 2019045932 (print) | LCCN 2019045933 (ebook) | ISBN 9781496441218 (hardcover) | ISBN 9781496444806 (trade paperback) | ISBN 9781496441225 (kindle edition) | ISBN 9781496441232 (epub) | ISBN 9781496441249 (epub)
Subjects: LCSH: Stiller, Karen. | Spouses of clergy—Biography.
Classification: LCC BV4395 .S75 2020 (print) | LCC BV4395 (ebook) | DDC 277.3/083092 [B]—dc23
LC record available at https://lccn.loc.gov/2019045932
LC ebook record available at https://lccn.loc.gov/2019045933

Printed in the United States of America

26   25   24   23   22   21   20
7   6   5   4   3   2   1

To Brent

*

Contents

Prologue *1*

1. Identity *5*
2. Doubt *21*
3. Community *41*
4. Marriage *59*
5. Family *75*
6. Friendship *93*
7. Funerals *109*
8. Envy *125*
9. Prayer *139*
10. Disappointment *157*
11. Forgiveness *169*
12. Christmas *183*
13. Moving *195*
14. Holiness *213*

Epilogue *233*

Acknowledgments 237
Notes 241
About the Author 245

PROLOGUE

MY HUSBAND, BRENT, AND I were on a weeklong vacation away from our three young kids, our busy work lives, and the dark, cold days of a Canadian winter. We had snatched up the last-minute deal online, taking advantage of visiting grandparents willing to be live-in babysitters. Soon after arriving, we met two other couples who became our fast friends at the Cuban resort. I don't remember now how we met, but I do remember the instant connection. I think we united around a shared aversion to walking on stilts or joining in on the Hula-Hoop competitions or any other group activities led by earnest resort staff. We had simply gotten along, and quickly.

We sat with them around the pool, reading those thick

paperback mysteries you take with you on vacation. We rented rickety bicycles from the resort and forced them up rutted dirt roads in the steaming heat, in search of yet another beach. Who knew the bikes would barely make it up a gentle hill? But on a rare tropical vacation in the company of lighthearted people, this just added to the fun.

A few evenings in, we shared a table for dinner at the resort restaurant, and as I excused myself to orbit the buffet yet again, I left everyone gabbing and laughing. When I returned just a few minutes later, plate piled high, they sat in silence, as if the lights had gone out in the conversation.

One look at Brent and I knew what had happened. "They finally asked what I do for a living," he said, attempting to break the awkwardness by naming the elephant that had lumbered into the room and now lounged at our table, huge and uncomfortable.

In previous conversations, the subject of work had never come up. But now they knew Brent was a pastor. At a church. And silence fell over the table. We had been having such a good time. I probably tried to say something funny, but nothing could have saved that dinner. We wrapped it up and called it a night.

The next day, one of the couples had grown colder than the January chill we were there to escape. All our laughter and banter screeched to a halt. The other couple broke open and leaned in close, as if they had just been waiting for a minister and his wife to show up on their vacation. Maybe they thought Brent had answers to some of their big questions about life and pain and God, some explanation for all that had befallen them. They trusted he would listen and care. He did, of course.

Our vacation time was drawing to a close by then, and we had only a couple more awkward days where we let the others set the tone while we mostly kept to ourselves. Not everyone wants to hang out with a pastor while on vacation.

The reactions of the two couples—one freezing over, the other warming up—are not unusual. Being a pastor, and being married to one, is a complicated life and vocation. People may put you on a pedestal: They assume you are better, nicer, kinder, and more holy than you are. Or they may skedaddle: They assume you are unkind and judgmental, or just weird.

Two of our new (now previous) friends must have thought we were there to judge them. They were married—but not to each other, as the old country song goes. We had just listened when they told us that early in the week. Maybe that was the moment when Brent should have told them he was a minister, but it would have felt so awkward, like we were either condoning or condemning when all we really wanted to do was snorkel and enjoy the beach, like everybody else.

* * *

"Is your life really like a fishbowl?" a friend once asked. He had heard this about ministers and their families, that people tap on the glass and peer in, hoping to see some stuff— maybe piles of laundry or two people yelling at each other.

And I guess they think we are watching them, too, and it makes them uncomfortable.

So yes, I told my friend that I do think some people watch us to see how very good or how very bad we are, and they make assumptions about us—what we are really like or how we will act. But even as some people watch us, I know that God watches *over* us. That is what I have learned. It's a very different kind of watching, and it is lovely.

CHAPTER I

Identity

Here is a trustworthy saying: Whoever aspires to be an overseer desires a noble task. Now the overseer is to be above reproach, faithful to his wife, temperate, self-controlled, respectable, hospitable, able to teach, not given to drunkenness, not violent but gentle, not quarrelsome, not a lover of money.

1 TIMOTHY 3:1-3

I THOUGHT we were going to Africa. That was our simple and beautiful plan. We dreamed of living and serving in a place where we could be useful and the good to be done felt huge, right there at your feet and at your fingertips. We longed to live somewhere vast, where love would be pulled and poured out of us and we could do as Jesus said, comforting widows and orphans and feeding hungry people and sheltering them with love and solid ceilings that would never leak. The last thing we wanted was a typical middle-class North American existence. We both loved to travel, and we were attracted to the simplicity of living where you didn't drown in plenty and where plenty didn't tempt you every single day.

We had both tasted that leaner life, just a nibble around the edges, before we met in university in 1988. Brent had been living wild and free in Burkina Faso, building fences around animals at a sanctuary and cataloging elephant dung for the scientists who lived at the wildlife preserve where he volunteered. I had just returned from the mountains of Colombia, where I had lived for a few months as part of a youth exchange program that helped me understand how large and gorgeous and painful the world really was—and that there was so much more of it beckoning me to explore. My life would forever stretch beyond North America, or so I hoped. I did not want my world to snap back to a size small.

As a newly married couple, we began to dream together about a future overseas, living simple, serving lives. When Brent completed his master of divinity degree in 1994 from a seminary in Vancouver, heading off to East Africa was a tender dream that seemed to be coming true.

Brent was going to help start a Bible college in Tanzania at the foot of Mount Kilimanjaro. In our minds, we were floating down a warm tropical river in the exact right direction. We met regularly with the man who had the vision for the college and dreamed about what was to come. Our undergraduate degrees in international development studies were still shiny and new, like our marriage certificate, and would be so useful—or so we thought. *We* were going to be so useful.

* * *

When you pursue an MDiv, you intern at a local church. It's the hands-on, practical side of the training. At the church where he was assigned, Brent helped the minister with various duties, like visiting the sick and elderly, running the Sunday school, preaching occasionally, and learning how churches work behind the scenes. He was also thrown headfirst into the drama that besieged this particular congregation, which involved a group of people who had grown discontented with their priest. It was a mutiny, like we were on a pirate ship.

My daydream of our little house in a land far away grew even more appealing because here was church gone wrong, right in front of my face. The minister and his wife confided in us over coffee breaks and dinners, and I could see how painful it all was for them.

A deep and deadly wound to their marriage began then, and they would eventually divorce. There was nothing appealing about what we were seeing. Africa still beckoned with her warm and welcoming hand.

But one Sunday during Brent's final year of study, I sat alone in my pew and observed him move around up front, doing liturgical and lovely things behind the altar as he helped set up for Communion. There is movement and order and precision in these visible parts of worship. This sacred art is passed on from priest to priest, and I was watching my husband's new friend, the minister so weary of his church's infighting, mentor Brent in these movements.

Just as he was receiving an education in church division,

Brent was being schooled in the objects of worship: things like fair white linen, with sharp creases ironed in by members of the chancel guild (a fierce army of older women you do not mess with), and the delicate silver cruet, polished to a high shine and slid into a purple velvet bag that is tied with a satin ribbon between Sunday appearances. It contains the water that is poured over the minister's hands just before he raises up a chunk of torn bread and says, "This is the body of Christ, broken for you."

Brent was learning that the burse goes on the veil goes on the pall goes on the paten goes on the purificator that drapes over the chalice that holds the wine brought to the people who are on their knees, hands held out to receive. And the minister is called to be right there in that black shirt and white collar, with his own past and future, and with how silly he can be and how loud he plays his music and how quickly he honks his horn in traffic, and with his own gigantic questions and unknowing, and yes, with his startled wife sitting there. Ministers know they have been asked to do this work, and all that comes with it. They have said yes to this call.

I watched. I could see that this leading of people into worship, and the provision of Communion itself, were beautiful and necessary to our lives in Christ. This beauty I was seeing was church, and it offered life. And just as clearly as if Jesus had slid into the pew beside me (late to arrive, but able to get away with that because people are just so relieved he showed up) and tugged me close and whispered with kindness in my ear, I knew Brent belonged in this exact kind of place, and that because we belonged together, so did I. We were not going to Africa. We were going to church.

As it turned out, Jesus whispered in Brent's ear, too, so my husband reached out to bishops who might take him on as a postulant—someone headed to the priesthood, on the track to ordination in the Holy Orders in the Anglican Church. Naturally, we were doing all this backward. You're supposed to have a bishop cheering you on before you enroll in seminary, not in your last year when God says, "No, sweethearts" to Tanzania.

Brent crafted his emails to the bishops, and I remained sad over losing my African dream. "I can live anywhere in Canada," I said to Brent, "but not Saskatchewan." I was young. I didn't know how beautiful that quiet, gentle province could be.

Three weeks later, we sold our last shred of cool—the beloved cherry-red Volkswagen camper van that had putt-putted into our hearts, up mountains, down into valleys, and through weekend camping trips filled with games of Scrabble in its musty old interior. We miss it still.

We crammed our belongings into an old gray Volvo station wagon that ultimately wouldn't handle the deep cold we were heading to any better than our old van could have. We spent our last minutes in Vancouver shoving dirty laundry into all the available crevices of our wagon and saying tearful goodbyes. The bishop who had tentatively decided to sponsor Brent in the ordained parish ministry wanted him immediately in the far reaches of, yes, Saskatchewan.

Brent became a minister. I became a minister's wife.

* * *

There was a funeral early on, Brent's first. It was for a tiny baby, a bloom of a girl who had barely lived. Her mother, a teenager, had selected a coffin covered in white faux fur, not much bigger than a shoebox. The coffin was on a small table at the front of the funeral home chapel. The baby's father, a teenage boy, stood outside behind a tree, and that is where he stayed.

When I walked into the chapel beside Brent, who wore his clerical collar for one of the first times, the funeral director bowed his head toward me and inquired as to whether I would play the organ. I said no. I didn't play the organ or any other instrument, but clearly there had been a minister's wife in the past who had.

But what was I doing there on that sad day, in that tragic room where it felt as if there were no air? It's not like I had to attend; it's not like ministers' spouses were required to show up at every wedding or funeral or come-and-go tea for Hank and Heather, fifty years married. I would have preferred to bolt and roam around town on that ugly day. But I wanted to support Brent. It was his job to keep it all together, to create and maintain a prayerful atmosphere, to move the family through this important ritual of goodbye and also to lead them in worship—because that also happens at funerals.

It is difficult to lead people in worship in the presence of a dead baby in a teeny coffin that is right beside you on a small table. I thought that this first funeral of Brent's might be one of the most difficult ones he would ever have, so I wanted to help him by being present with a calm assurance. I wanted him to be able to glance down when he needed to and see a loving, nodding face encouraging and reassuring him. I would be strong for him.

I sobbed through the entire funeral. I burst into tears with the first strains of the slow, sad country ballad about a dream being just like a river, and from there I could not stop, not even for a minute. Brent avoided looking at me.

When I thought it could not get any worse, we went to a small reception at the home of the teenage mom and her parents and brothers and sisters, the place where her bedroom was just down the hall, with all her teenage stuff and maybe even a crib she and her dad had already assembled. I did not want to go. Sitting through the saddest funeral in Saskatchewan was bad enough, but to voluntarily sit down at the same round table as grief, eat a sandwich across from sorrow, and drink tea from great-grandmother's dainty cups full of anguish would all be too much. I preferred to forget— or maybe never learn—that babies' lives can end so quickly. And I was terrified of the stupid things I might say. What if I accidentally asked about the boy behind the tree?

But I went anyway. I had to. Brent had to. It wasn't about us. It was about showing up and walking straight in the door, even though I was full of fear. I took my lead from Brent and said safe things only—"I'm so sorry. And yes, please, I will have more tea. This is a beautiful cup."

* * *

I notice other ministers' wives. I'm curious about how they carry out their roles, how front-and-center they are, even what they are wearing. Almost always, I think they are doing it better than I am. Some women seem to have a knack. I visited a church in Florida where the minister's wife sat in the very first row, where it seemed to me you couldn't get away with any twitching, sneaking a look at your phone, or refereeing wars between your children, who are the worst-behaved children in church. That's why I never sit that close to the front.

When this woman's husband wrapped things up and was about to recess out—in that church and in ours, the clergy file in during the processional and file out during the recessional, like a parade—the minister paused as he passed his wife's pew and offered her his hand. She stood, and they marched out together, arms pumping. Jaunty. Maybe they just couldn't wait to get to lunch, but it seemed like more than that to me. It seemed like an announcement: "She's with me! I'm with him!" The congregation beamed at them as they walked by and seemed proud of their couple.

It struck me that this is not something Brent and I would ever do. I could not pull that off, and Brent would never pull me out of my seat. That is one way of doing things, but it is not our way. He has always told whatever church he serves that I am his wife but also simply another member of the congregation—we are not a "buy one get one free" deal. I would be myself and figure out my place in the community like everybody else.

In some ways, this approach has not worked at all. People still think you are a little more together than normal, or I guess they hope you are because your husband is up there preaching all the time about good and holy things, about surviving the world and how to love it well. They think you know how to turn the church photocopier on and why kids get cancer, and that you want to say grace at the annual spaghetti dinner when your husband is home with a fever. They haven't seen your closet or inside your cupboards, although if you leave certain people alone in your kitchen, they will look. They haven't heard you yell, and they don't know what you did when you were seventeen and then again at twenty-two because you cannot learn your lesson the first time, but only the hard way. They haven't seen inside your heart, which is as confused as anyone else's. If anything, the expectation people have that a minister's wife might be more on the spiritual ball than the average bear has made me even more aware of my flaws—and my claws.

But not all expectations are bad. Some save you. For me, one is the expectation that I will be there and belong. That I will show up and be part of this faith and of this or that church—big or small, east or west, city or country—year after year, hardly missing a beat and rarely a Sunday, and never a good rummage sale. Showing up and choosing to belong have been ways I have loved my husband well and learned to love God better, and certainly the people who bug me. To belong is a discipline that helps me to believe. The conviction I have that I need to appear at church—and probably not every minister's spouse feels this way—has tethered me when I might have otherwise floated away, as the best-hearted people sometimes do.

I have seen enough people drift away from their faith to know that holding on to mine is what is best for me. And church, with all its imperfections, is faith's incubator. Church is faith's hospital and its picnic grounds, its sheltering tree and also the rich soil from which it grows. Church embraces faith and holds it tenderly with strong arms. It embraces me. And so I love the church, even when it expects more of me than I think it should.

But there are some expectations that make you sit up straighter and occasionally iron your shirt—which makes you feel neat and tidy. These are expectations that help you attend to your soul and abide. Abiding is big. Jesus tells his fickle, frightened followers to abide in him, and he promises that he will abide in them. It is that simple and that hard. This is the deal Jesus and I have struck together: I will stay put. I abide.

* * *

Jessie is a mom in our church. One day she asked whether I could help her by picking up her son Max from school and keeping him company for a few hours while she went to an appointment. Jessie is in her twenties and crochets shawls in sky blues and deep grassy greens. She is our church's unofficial dancer, swaying and lifting her bare arms into the air and twirling her hands as if she were a ballerina, but better. Max's little brother, Nico, is attached to Jessie with a beautiful woven cloth knotted to her waist in a way that makes me inwardly cluck with worry. He never falls out, though. Jessie knows what she is doing.

I say yes to lending a hand with Max, who is a first-grade stick of dynamite. He is all yells and bluster, charging from spot to spot. I hold my breath whenever he gallops up the side aisle of the church at full speed, ducking and darting around ladies; one time he ran straight into a pillar in a Sunday school room, which did slow him down for a second.

On Friday I arrived at the school's side gate on Lockhart Road with my dog, Dewey, a large and playful goldendoodle. It had been years since I picked up someone else's young child at school, and I was nervous. The last time I was supposed to do it, I forgot. First the principal's office called me, then Ben's mother. But on this day I was on time, and with my happy dog. I had brought Dewey because I thought Max would like him. I wanted Max to enjoy the celebrity-level attention that routinely happens when accompanying my dog in public places.

Before Max came out, head bobbing along in the river of kids flowing from the school, the teacher at the side gate grilled me as we stood beside the big red sign that said, "No Dogs Allowed." I told her I was there to pick up Max, the son of a friend.

"Do you have a note from his mother?" she asked me.

"No, I don't," I answered.

"Will Max have a note from his mother?"

"I have no idea," I replied. "I hope so."

She told me I couldn't take Max without a note.

"Well, let's wait and see," I said, and prayed that Max would have a note.

Then he was there at my side, wearing his giant backpack like a turtle in his shell. He clutched a soccer ball and hopped from one foot to the other. One skinny arm squeezed Dewey's head in a side hug. Max had a note.

Then, "This is my priest's wife!" he bellowed. "This is my priest's wife!"

People swiveled to look. A hush seemed to fall on the entire surrounding neighborhood. The teacher who asked for the note looked sheepish and said, "I'm sorry."

"Don't be," I said. "It's good you have that rule."

Why is she apologizing?

I thought I knew. I am a minister's wife, so I must be more reliable and honest than the average complete stranger. And wasn't it silly, and didn't she feel awkward requiring documentation from a *minister's wife* to take a child who was not her own from the schoolyard?

"It's a miracle I even remembered to come. I'm no more reliable or better than you are," I wanted to say. This was the lonely, set-apart place of ministry that I found confusing. It is Jesus who is good and reliable and never late and always shows up. The rest of us are just stumbling behind together.

I was right to bring Dewey. We walked to my car with Max calling out, "Look! Look at this dog! He's my friend! Look!" to the kids boarding buses or crying or getting in trouble with their mothers already.

At my house, Max was too busy to have the snack I offered, and he jumped quickly into a chat about Catholicism, because why not?

"Is Brent our pope?" Max asked me.

"Nope," I answered. It was Brent's day off, and he spent much of Max's visit collapsed on the red couch in our living room. I was glad he wasn't our pope, because what would Max think then?

Max, in fact, seemed quite comfortable in our house and not at all thrown by Brent and all his loafing—more comfortable than I would have been as a kid entering the mysterious realm of the minister's home.

Our family attended church almost every Sunday when I was a child. It seemed everyone went to church back then. It was weird if you didn't go. Now it's weird if you do.

One day I was in the white clapboard house, the manse that had housed so many ministers and their families. The house stood alone on the edge of the church parking lot, set apart, across from the graveyard where my older sister Miriam and I would sometimes wander, diligent not to step on the grass where we thought the bodies were buried.

I always lingered for a chilling moment at the grave site of the children called the Babes in the Woods, two sisters who had died in 1842, lost in the forest that was now subdivisions and schools, the bowling alley and the Kmart. Their deaths puzzled me. How had this safe suburbia, so known and predictable to me, been a place of such peril? And it was impossible to imagine my sister—who, as part of her weekly routine, would pin me down and drool on my glasses—holding me tenderly in the cold as the two of us curled up together under a tree, dying. But then we would tear out through the narrow metal gates together, lighter on our feet than before, simply from realizing we were still alive and breathing.

The ministers' families lived a stone's throw from that graveyard until they started buying their own houses to avoid the poverty that always seemed to come with retirement. It fascinated me to wander around that house, now used for church meetings and Sunday school activities—which must have been the reason I was there. There was a kitchen, proof that ministers' families ate like other people. There was a washroom, of course, and it shocked me there would be a gleaming white porcelain toilet in a house built for ministers. Somehow I had not realized that our minister used the bathroom. It jolted me. How could someone holy be so bodily? Did the minister bellow for more toilet paper like my dad did?

Somewhere around that time, I started to become friends with Marian, our minister's daughter. I remember kind and quiet Mrs. Dempsey, Marian's mother and the only minister's wife from my childhood that I can recall. I couldn't imagine her playing bridge in our living room with my mother, holding court at her card table. My mom smoked cigarettes and owned a glittery jumpsuit that made her look exotic for our town. My mom drank rye whiskey and 7UP and yakked on the phone that hung on one of the bright orange walls in the kitchen she cursed daily for being so small. She sang old camp songs when we drove long distances, cajoling my sister and me to sing along, which we did. My mother led sing-alongs on our class trips, a reliable chaperone who came along whenever she could and always brought the fun, like it was packed in her big purse.

Now I know that Mrs. Dempsey must have been as full of mystery, beauty, and battle as any other mother. But I didn't know that then. Maybe she and my mom would have been great friends, if they had allowed themselves.

At our house, on the day of Max's visit, I gave him the run of the place. I think he liked being there, rattling through our saved LEGOs, pulling out this and that and piecing them together. He exploded through closed doors, peeked in drawers, and grilled me about anything that crossed his mind.

Downstairs, Max ripped open the Star Wars Risk game I had spent too much money on one Christmas. No one here will ever touch it. "Go ahead, Max," I said.

The next Sunday at church, Max was down front receiving Communion. I watched him. He was a little bird trembling at the rail, ready to fly off and get back to busy. Max raised his right arm and crossed himself, left to right and back again, with a vigor and energy rarely seen in that simple, holy action. I was glad I was a witness.

CHAPTER 2

Doubt

....

When they saw him, they worshiped him; but some doubted.

MATTHEW 28:17

I OPENED MY HEART to faith and faith opened her arms to me, in the living room of my childhood home, alone on a Friday night at 25 Windward Avenue in Dartmouth, Nova Scotia. I was going to university, and I lived with my parents. It wasn't that I hadn't believed in God before that night. I had, in a vague way. But in the church I grew up in, it felt like things were mostly about safe, friendly God—a slightly anonymous fellow, like the jovial man down the street who waves to you out the window as you cut across his lawn. Just barely there in your life, hardly noticeable. I had not paid much attention to Jesus in particular. He appealed to me with his beard and kind eyes, and he often seemed to be holding a sweet lamb. Jesus was simply the main character in a lot of the more pleasant biblical stories. God on the go. Except for the sad bits of Holy Week, of course; but those were more like an annual blip.

Brent had broken up with me just a few weeks earlier, so I suppose my heart was exhausted, vulnerable, and ready for something new and nice. After four months of dating, I had told Brent I loved him. Never one to soften a blow, at least not back then (this happening long before his pastoral training on how to deliver bad news kindly), he said, "I don't love you, and I don't think I ever will."

It's difficult to bounce back relationally from that.

He was wrong, of course. He would love me, but neither of us knew that then.

The night he ended things, I left the little vegetarian restaurant where we had been eating and headed back over the bridge that linked Halifax to Dartmouth, the city he lived in with the city I lived in. If he was never going to love me back, I might as well go buy cigarettes. So I did.

I also worked my summer job at a local brewery and flirted with an American sailor named John, and Brent briefly dated a girl named Twyla, which I've never really forgotten.

Still, I missed Brent and his scratchy golden beard and the smell and sound of him. I missed his mind and how he challenged me on almost everything. I felt very bad, wandering around alone at the bottom of things. So I made an appointment with Andrew, my parents' minister, the nice man who had made church seem slightly more interesting to me, even before I met Brent.

I respected Andrew. He had gotten into trouble in South Africa for protesting apartheid before he landed in what must have seemed like Ordinaryville, where my parents and I lived.

"I'm confused," I said to Andrew. "I thought Brent was the man God had chosen for me."

He looked at me across his big wooden desk and said, "He might still be the man God has picked out for you."

In the weeks that followed, I thought about my faith and about how much of it I had accepted because of all my years in Sunday school during my childhood, and how much of it I had believed because of the cute guy I had met. I had to decide whether it was something I was going to fully accept for myself and whether I would allow it to change my life. I was very open then, in my sadness.

That night, I looked around the familiar living room, which hadn't changed much over the years, even though I had changed. Gold-flecked mirror tiles still covered one wall—handy for perfecting our dance moves as teenagers, but now reflecting a young woman sitting alone. The low windows could still be pushed open so you could lie on the orange carpet and blow cigarette smoke out over the garden in a manner that was never as sneaky as you presumed. The TV was in the same corner, but I didn't turn it on or even bother with any lights.

"If you're real, please show up," I prayed, or something like that. And I experienced something in response. Jesus did show up, gently, like a butterfly. I sank into faith, as if I had leaned back into a pile of feather pillows on my bed and sighed.

It was a wave of love. I was not alone.

Love showed up in the room, like a neighbor with a lemon meringue pie, unexpected and so very welcome. Love impressed itself upon me in a way it had not before, and I was certain that it all was real.

I recognized the love in the room as a love that I could not damage or push away. This love would love me back and love me first and love me more and love me still, and I was caught up in it wholly. God made things beautifully personal, kind, and tender.

"Thank you," I said, this time out loud. It was all still a bit formal then, as things are at the beginning of almost everything that turns out to be important. But then I experienced a warmth that was like the deepest of embraces, wrapping around me and patching me simultaneously. My heart perked up and began to sit up straight and look around again. My heart was revived. And then I said, "Yes."

That was my first yes, which led to an instant belief. But it also placed me on the road of a lifetime of believing over and over again. Conversion can happen in a moment, yes, but it is also a continual process of turning toward what is true and saying, "Okay. Please. Oh, thank you." I believed, but I was only beginning to believe. I became like new, but not completely quite yet. I sensed even on this night that faith would not be easy but would be worth it: beautiful and hard.

It was all still as mysterious as the night, but also as plain as the day. You don't need to have everything figured out in the first moments, or maybe even ever. I recognized that

Jesus was true and real and alive, as we sing so joyfully in Easter hymns, and not just flat between pages in a book for children, winsome with a lamb.

One belief led to another that night, in a kind of spiritual cascade. That's how it happened for me. I understood for the first time the language of spiritual rebirth. God reached down and gently turned me around, like someone who loves you does, touching your shoulder and pivoting you toward the beautiful thing you are missing because something distracted you and turned you around the other way.

On our family vacations, I was the girl in the back seat of the car with my nose in a book. "Look, Karen!" my mother would say as a deer bounded across the road or a black bear prowled on the shoulder of the highway. I would swivel my head and frantically scan the landscape out the window, hoping to catch a glimpse.

"Where? Where? Where?" I would miss everything, all the good stuff. I was always too late. I made my family crazy.

But that night, a kind touch pointed me exactly in the right direction. I could see.

I was well on my way to the new and fresh air of belief. If Jesus had actually been born, then died and rose again, it mattered. It meant something for the world generally, yes, but also for me specifically. And if all that was true, then I should pay special attention to the things Jesus had said—crucial things about being the Truth and the Life, the Bread and the Water, the Way. He also told us to love our neighbors as ourselves, to put God above the other yearnings in our lives. He said he was our one true love and the answer to all our yearning. My true love. The answer to all of my yearning.

Of course, I'm still learning all this. Conversion takes a second and a lifetime. Amazingly, you can experience all this wonder and still be a jerk.

But I did see that the world was painted in colors I had not previously noticed, a masterpiece in which I stood in the corner, amazed.

* * *

Soon after the night that changed my heart, I trotted off to confirmation classes at my parents' church, led by Andrew. Confirmation is when baptized people publicly proclaim their faith in front of the church. The classes prepare them for this significant step and are usually filled with young teenagers.

I had been confirmed years earlier, but since I was a new me, I decided to do it all over again. "Which part of the Bible is more important—the old or the new?" asked Andrew during the first class.

I shot my arm straight up like I was in fourth grade. The younger people around me knew a trick church question when they heard one. "The New Testament!" I shouted out.

Andrew replied as kindly as he could. "Actually, Karen, they are equally important." For safety's sake, I quieted down and listened through the rest of the classes and learned what Christians like me had believed for centuries.

I devoured every class. I was given a structure for the love that had gripped me that night, like being handed a proper and sturdy hanger for a beautiful new dress. Weeks after the first class, on a Sunday morning, I stood in front of the church of my childhood and said the words "I believe" for everyone to hear. And a few months after that I bumped into Brent on the Halifax waterfront, crowded with tourists on a beautiful Saturday afternoon. I tried to remain aloof, but it was no use. I started to smile almost immediately—and so did he.

*   *   *

Years later, as a minister's wife, I knelt to receive wine from the cup that is part of Communion on a Sunday morning. I admired my new short haircut, reflected in the polished side of the big silver chalice in the server's hands. I'm sure the server would have been as surprised as I was that I was using the chalice as a mirror.

My new life in Christ felt old on that day, I guess. Instead of pondering the great sacrifice Jesus had made for me on the cross and how much and how freely I had been forgiven, I thought about how much I really did like my new look.

Sometimes worship moves us, and sometimes it does not. Sometimes our love is in order, and sometimes it is in disarray. Sometimes I believe it all, and sometimes I feel like I do not.

Faith is like that. Some days it is a tiny bird that comes to the window and then flies off for a while. I have decided that is okay. What I feel doesn't change what is true, after all.

*   *   *

We have three children—Erik, Holly, and Thomas—and now they are almost grown. They have been raised up seated down Sunday mornings on straight-backed wooden pews, dad at the front, mother to the side. They have been reared with the church at the center and all around them; with spaghetti dinners and Bible studies, choir parties and meetings that lasted too long, and trays of leftover sandwiches brought home from funeral receptions. Our children are of potlucks and prayer meetings, hymnbooks and late nights on Christmas Eve, waiting for Brent to get home. They have run laughing and screeching like monkeys through empty churches and halls after everyone else left to go home a full hour before. Church is their friend and family, their mild annoyance and great comfort, and the messy place and sweet grace which they are from.

When our youngest son, Thomas, was three, he pulled down his shorts and peed on the side of the church. I was sure it wasn't the first time he had picked this target; he had reveled in the freedom of going anywhere, anytime—a phase nearly all boys go through. I just hadn't caught him yet, so I hadn't created a rule about it. I seemed to need rules for so many things. It struck me as completely, 100 percent not allowed—ever—especially for one of the minister's boys. "From now on," I said, "only and ever at our house, and preferably in the bathroom."

This was our son who always pulled or pushed in the opposite direction. Our daring risk taker. We had named him Thomas, after the disciple in the Bible who said he wouldn't believe Jesus was alive after the Crucifixion until he could see and touch Jesus' hands and side for himself.

I've always liked that story and that disciple. Jesus said, "Put your finger here," and Thomas did believe, deeply and for the rest of his life; but only after seeing the wounds firsthand. Then he became a supermissionary. Thomas had the courage to ask and admit how deeply he doubted, right there in the midst of a group of people who all believed more than he did—or appeared to. Their stronger faith didn't intimidate him. Really, they were probably all terrified at what was happening around them in those days. His demand for proof would have helped everybody. Thomas the brave and the real.

Doubt is not the shadow of faith, after all. Doubt is faith's most faithful companion. We should listen to what doubt says and say things back, like "Oh, come right in. Stop hiding outside behind that bush" and "Look, everybody, who I just found." Doubt can be brought out into the light, where maybe a person can find an answer or two or learn to better live with mystery.

Jesus says that people should become like little children to enter the Kingdom of Heaven. Before I had children, I did not know children well, so I thought Jesus meant we needed to become sweet—to be trusting and compliant and believe nicely whatever we were told, to sit quietly with what we were given.

After I had children, I realized they are not all that sweet. They question everything—at least mine did. They ask why. They ask how, what, and when, and then they start all over again. They don't question their right to ask or think their questions are inappropriate. They're not embarrassed yet. They ask so persistently and so loudly that you don't even know what to do with them after a while. *What will make them stop asking so many questions?* you wonder, hiding in the bathroom.

* * *

I was leading a women's Bible study in the basement of one of my husband's churches. I wasn't required to do this as part of my minister's-wife role, even though some people might have thought so. I enjoyed helping these groups get going for the sake of having fellowship with other women and for the accountability of reading the Bible in a consistent way for months at a time. These groups helped me. They built my faith. The women and their questions and answers sustained and stretched me. I also enjoyed the small cakes and the lemon squares. Ladies' groups always do snacks well, and drinking tea from the porcelain cups that are stacked up in church basements everywhere is a pleasant thing to do.

The verse we were studying that day from 2 Peter touched on the matter of angels behaving badly. It said something uncomfortable about God not sparing angels when they sinned but putting them in gloomy pits. No one knew what that meant. And it sounded awful, like when someone you love suddenly starts saying harsh things, and you wonder, *What just happened?*

For a moment I wished I had been somewhere else, because sometimes as the minister's wife you are expected to have special insight because of whom you are married to. If you are married to a plumber, do people expect you to grab a wrench and crawl under the kitchen sink?

So I said, "I don't understand that. It sounds weird." The verse felt complicated, and the idea of angels as I normally imagined them being sent to pits of any kind was difficult to reconcile.

A few women started to laugh, and one of them said, "Oh, Karen," and another said, "I love you." I knew she was saying it lightly, but I also knew she was saying it deeply. I had reminded her it was okay to not know, to think something is strange and incomprehensible, and that we don't need to have everything so perfectly laid out and nailed down all the time—even if you're a minister's wife.

I believed that sharing my questions and my doubts could lighten things up quite a bit. If I could admit those things, the other women at the Bible study certainly could. If we shared and discussed them, we might unravel the mystery, or just be more content abiding in it together. It was okay; we didn't need to panic.

It is okay not to know. It is okay to sometimes think some things are weird. This is one thing I believe all the time.

* * *

The arm of Saint Francis Xavier, the patron saint of missionaries, recently visited the city where I live. I am not Roman Catholic, but when I read in the newspaper that a Catholic group had brought the 465-year-old severed arm of one of their most beloved saints to Ottawa for display at the Notre

Dame Cathedral, I wanted to see it. My daughter, Holly, came with me. She is my companion in all things adventurous and spiritual—when she's not annoyed with me, as nineteen-year-old daughters can be with their mothers.

Saint Francis baptized thousands of people in Asia before he died from fever on the mission field in China. For being so old, the arm looks surprisingly youthful. Yes, it is grayish green, but it is not a skeleton, which is what you might expect. The Catholic ritual of veneration, or honoring a saint (usually by visiting a shrine or viewing a relic), is an ancient practice. I've never fully understood the Catholic view of saints, but I have friends who are Catholic and have done acts of veneration, and I respect them. They would have liked that I was going, and they probably wouldn't have swiveled their heads around as I did, taking notes.

"Enjoy your time in prayer," said the woman up front, one of the organizers of the event. She explained that hundreds of years ago people couldn't travel as far as they do today, so the Catholic church would bring these artifacts to the faithful.

I appreciated how she was explaining everything so clearly and calmly, as if there were nothing particularly unusual happening—just another day with a very old arm. Then she declared the time of visitation officially open. "And don't knock it over," she added. "We don't want to be the city that knocks Saint Francis's arm over." She also asked us not to kiss the glass box containing the arm, because it was flu season.

Holly and I made our way slowly from the very back row of the cathedral. When we first arrived at the church that day, we had avoided the empty seats near the front because we were Protestants doing this definitely non-Protestant thing. After all, what if a giant Catholic spotlight were to suddenly swing on us and show everyone that we had no idea what we were doing?

So we had sat in the back, and it was a long, slow walk to the front. There was a young man in the balcony who played a guitar and sang worship songs. His voice drifted through the cathedral, lovely and soft: "Holy, holy, holy! Lord God Almighty! Early in the morning our song shall rise to thee."

Finally, we were only a few steps away from the relic placed on the altar. The arm itself was nestled in what could best be described as its own arm-shaped dish, silver and beautiful and encased in a rectangular glass box. The ushers had given us a prayer card when we first arrived that depicted Saint Francis Xavier on one side with a prayer on the other. We were told we could touch the card to the box and say a prayer or simply ask for healing from God for whatever we wanted. *Everything*, I said in my mind as I touched the small card to the box. Everything was the only thing I could think of as I did this thing I probably would not be doing again.

We made our way back down the side aisle of the church under the astonishing stained-glass windows and the deep blue of the ceiling—painted like a night sky with yellow stars the color of marigolds—and then out a side door into the freezing-cold air.

I felt a lightness of being for the rest of the day, a beautiful calm. I floated back to our SUV parked on a side road, filthy with dirty snow grime, empty candy bags on the floor, and shoe prints on the dash—even though I've asked a thousand times.

"Catholics are lucky. They get all this extra stuff," Holly said, and then asked me if I had time for a coffee. I was thankful for our special relationship and joyful that my daughter wanted to spend even more time with me. "Yes!" I said. The day just kept getting better. Then her phone pinged, and she changed her mind almost immediately and had me drop her off at the corner to meet a friend instead.

But still, I felt light. What millions of mysteries this world must contain that cannot be solved or even properly named. This day my faith was fed, and my spirit relaxed from being tied up in knots like a backache, as it sometimes is.

Later that night, I was at our church's Friday-night drop-in program. At 7:30 we open the doors, and a regular group of people stream in and sit around small tables to eat hot soup and sandwiches and socialize. These are our friends who live close to the edge of things. Our job is to serve the food and visit, if we think a person wants company.

We begin by carrying around a big yellow plastic bowl of potato chips, handing out individual portions with tongs. The chips are a popular item, not only for our guests but also for those of us in the kitchen. It's tough to stop eating them. We follow with homemade soup made by church members, then sandwiches, and we finish off the night with the pleasantness of ice cream sandwiches around 9:30.

Our friends talk in small groups, play euchre, knit, flip through magazines they have brought with them, and maybe ask for a sandwich with no mayonnaise.

Sometimes people ask for prayer before they leave. It might be to find a lost cell phone or a lost son. Once a month, there is a worship service held in the church's library.

That night, after my experience at the cathedral, I chatted with a man whom I had never seen before at our Friday-night program. He towered over me and had a tremendous head of dark hair. He reminded me of my father, if my father had lived a more difficult life. He told me he comes to our church only on the Fridays when there is a church service after supper. On Sundays, he attends the Catholic church around the corner.

"I went to see Saint Francis's arm today!" I said. My new friend hadn't heard about this, and he peppered me with questions: "What arm?" and "Whose arm?" and "Why?"

As I recounted everything to this Catholic who surely must get this arm business more than I do, it sounded a bit crazy to my ears. The initial bloom of good feeling that had lifted me up since leaving the cathedral wilted like a cut flower, as these things do. The man listened closely. "I can see the love in you. I can see that you are a woman of God," he told me when I finished. "I can just see it!" he said in his warm voice. It was so loud I glanced around uncomfortably to see who else was listening.

I told him, a little more quietly, "I can see it in you too," because I could. His love for God was there in his eyes, and

I could feel devotion coming from him like warmth from a campfire. In our church, we believe a saint is anyone who has been rescued by God and sees that. This man was a saint to me, so alive and very well, standing in front of me.

Eventually about a dozen people walked down the hall to the library, leaving the rest of the group eating and gabbing. We sang some hymns, and then one of the guests stood up to read from the book of Revelation. The man read carefully and precisely. The passage mentioned something about people singing. He surprised us by suddenly singing those very verses. His voice was quavering and out of tune, but what do I know? He was brave, and I found it beautiful. He abandoned himself to the words in front of him in a way that I just couldn't imagine happening on a Sunday morning, when people are better dressed, with matching socks.

Then Pastor Michelle, a priest at our church who grew up like a flower in Kentucky, preached a sermon about telling people about Jesus. She smiled and said, "Why wouldn't you tell others when you have this amazing news to share?"

God was there in that little room on that cold night, tending to our ragged and ripped hearts. My tall friend with the spectacular hair sat across the room from me. We smiled at each other. I was thankful he had reminded me I was a woman of God.

* * *

The Bible is full of God reminding people to remember. *Remember when things were good. Remember when you sensed me near. Remember that time I showed up and you could almost see me. Remember the manna, right there on the ground at your feet, ready for pickup. Remember the bird at the window and your parents' living room.* Our holy memories sustain and fill us, like bread warm from the oven. Remembering soothes and sustains and nudges us back to faith.

When I feel alone or lose the desire to pray, I try to do this holy work of remembering. I try to remember all that I do know instead of what I do not.

If I meet someone who seems like a minister's wife who does not choose her Sunday morning clothes solely based on what does not need to be ironed, I can feel intimidated and forget that God told me quite a while ago that I was just fine, and that I would also grow. I have to remind myself that I am loved completely and forever—and that on a long-ago night in my parents' living room, I would not have doubted that, not even for a second.

A lot about life is just so ordinary: buying new shoelaces because ours are frayed and tired, opening the refrigerator in the morning and realizing there is no milk for breakfast, and walking our dogs more slowly as they age.

So much about our faith lives can feel ordinary too. Most of us don't live on the top of a mountain, and the arm of a saint doesn't swing through town very often. Men with great hair don't remind us very often, in big warm voices, of exactly who we are. Easter morning, with its lilies heavy in their own perfume, dawns only once a year.

Instead, we drag ourselves out of bed and clean up messes that reappear almost instantly. Our floors are dusty and our hair turns gray. But yes, we do have these extraordinary moments—and maybe even entire seasons—when we know so clearly that God loves us, and that it's true. We forget, but then we can remember.

* * *

The next Sunday at church, our friend Doug was up front reading Scripture as the kids stormed out and charged to Sunday school. They push and laugh in their rowdy line, and the person assigned to the first reading sometimes hesitates in the face of this uprising. It's a bit awkward. A scuffle might break out over who gets to carry the small wooden cross, or the offering basket is yanked from hand to hand while we're all there watching.

Wisely, Doug launched in anyway and read the Old Testament passage from Genesis 12 about the calling of Abram, who would be renamed Abraham. God shows up out of the deep blue and asks Abram to leave everything he knows and follow him into the wilderness. He promises his uncertain follower that he will eventually have as many descendants as the stars in the sky.

I know Doug and his wife, Carolyn, a little bit. Brent and I had dinner at their house, and we ate a lot of cheese for four people. They also served steaming beef bourguignonne out of their Crock-Pot, tender and delicious. We laughed, mostly about what terrible parents we had sometimes been and how much of a miracle it was that our kids—six between us—seemed to be turning out okay despite us.

Doug is a kind man, and faithful. Although we didn't talk about it that night, I assume he has doubts and dry times in his faith, just like everybody else, and that he would not be shocked to hear about the times I feel far from God. He might even be relieved.

We all hold each other up and in. Together we walk this long, slow path of conversion—a lifetime of moments sinking into what is so plain and what is so mysterious.

If Doug had kept reading that day in church, we would have reached the part of Abraham's story years later when he and his wife, Sarah—who had encountered God in an amazing, literal, right-in-your-face manner—begin to doubt. They question whether and how God will ever give them that one son they need to kick things off, to be that first promised burst of light in the sky. And the thing is—for me, for Doug, and definitely for Abraham—God does show up again eventually. Memory and faith return.

CHAPTER 3

Community

*Let us consider how we may spur one another on toward love
and good deeds, not giving up meeting together, as some are in
the habit of doing, but encouraging one another—and all the
more as you see the Day approaching.*

HEBREWS 10:24-25

I DID NOT INHERIT my mother's beautiful singing voice. I am
a terrible singer.

One morning at church, I sat in the very last row. On that
Sunday, the choir sang from the back, lined up as neat as pins
behind me. This small but beautiful choir was directed by
two retired opera singers—a married couple who, once every
few Sundays, created this miracle for all of us.

The choir was known in town for the depth of their can-
tatas and the height of their descants—and for their understanding that people like me would never attempt to join.
In some small way, I believed the group's singing ability
reflected well on me as a minister's wife, and I took pride in

them, a group of singers I would not have been able to bribe my way into.

With the piano's prelude cue, the choir began the first stanza of "Holy, Holy, Holy! Lord God Almighty!" As I listened to the beauty and strength of their voices, each separate strand blending perfectly with the others to create this magnificent thing, I thought, *Yes, God is holy! He must be, because would you just listen to that?*

The entire congregation joined in on the second stanza, so I did too—a bit slow and low coming out of the gates, just croaking along like normal. My bad best. Yet because I was physically so close to the assembled singers, right there in front of them with one of the sopranos singing almost into my ear, I became one of them for a few brief moments. My confidence rose. So did my voice. I sang louder and louder—and at least to my ears, better and better.

I was in their midst. They carried me, and changed me. I improved because they were there behind me. They took me exactly as I was and helped transform me, because I was part of them. And I knew this thing I was part of had everything to do with God and worship and community.

That is church. This is what it is and what it does. It helps us welcome each other, carry each other. It helps point us to holiness and move us that way together, toward that warm light. It is all our brokenness pointed and moving in the same direction.

In church, we arrive broken and then are put back together,

like beautiful vases fallen off a high shelf. To be broken and to know it means you are aware of who you really are in your deepest and darkest places. Brokenness means that pretending to be deeply good and wonderfully wonderful is over, if you were ever able to pull that act off in the first place. Pretending is impossible because your cracks and dried glue are showing.

To be broken in this churchy way means being grateful and unashamed. This is because you know it is Jesus who picked you up after that bad fall. He picked you up and pieced you back together and placed you back up in a safe place, and then he gave you flowers to hold as well, just to be kind. You may have been badly broken, but now you are beautiful.

I know so many people who have dropped out of church and away from community of this kind. Everyone knows someone who just doesn't have time for it anymore. Something bad happened at church, or another member did something stupid and mean to them, or things are just crazy busy with their kids and their cats. I once met a woman who stopped coming because someone had sat in her pew.

We can hurt each other, but I think those who have left are missing something important. They have left behind something full of imperfections and full of the potential of love.

* * *

One time Thomas had a hockey tournament out of town on a Sunday morning. We were very awful to our kids and didn't allow Sunday-morning activities that weren't church related.

But this was a rare occurrence and a big game—plus he was our third child, and by then sometimes you give up a little bit. I drove Thomas to the arena a few towns over. I had time before the game began, so I went to the coffee shop across the road with my book.

It was a revelation. The place was full of people enjoying themselves with their coffee and newspapers. Entire families were there with their kids not fighting. Everyone appeared to be having a lovely morning.

I opened my book with a sigh of satisfaction. I realized this must be what Sunday morning is like for other people. It turns out that while I'm in church, people are going out for walks and talks. Or they are reading alone with their tea or coffee, and maybe sneaking a donut stuffed with jelly, because they deserve one after the week they've had.

No one had to bribe or blackmail their kids to get there on time. No one stole a glance at their phone to see what time it was and calculate how much longer they'd have to sit in their booth with their jelly donut. And no one had to talk to the person next to them or put up with them at all, or so it seemed to me.

I felt a bit jealous, thinking about Sunday mornings in our house. The threats. Sometimes the dread. We go to church almost every Sunday, all the time, all year round. The minister's wife, at least the way I do minister's wife-ing, does not miss the Sunday service unless her leg is broken. And the leg would have to have broken that very morning.

It's not like we always want to go to church. The service can feel too long. Sometimes the songs drag, the sermon stinks, and the people can be really annoying. They gather around and ask how you are and how your week's been—when you've had a crappy one and don't want to share one little bit. And there is always someone available to tell you that you look tired, even though you put makeup on and actually ironed your shirt.

Sometimes, because I'm the minister's wife, they will pass along comments to me, wanting me to pass them on to Brent—or so I must assume. Once I had to ask someone to stop doing that, because it was too painful to hear her complaints—the guitars were fine, but the drums were too loud and the sermons too long. "Your husband doesn't listen very well," she said.

"Please just stop," I said to her over the phone on a day when neither of us should have been talking to each other. Things got heated and loud. I should have hung up then, but I didn't. I kept going. I wonder why we can't just stop, when the stop sign is right there clearly in front of us at the intersection?

I told Brent about it later. "Yeah, it sounds like things got carried away. It's too bad," he said.

Weeks passed. My anger melted. My shame grew. A deep sense that I needed to apologize and make things right grew up in anger's place, along with amazement that I had actually said the things I had said. I liked this woman, and I knew I had hurt her.

"You should do what you think is right," confirmed Brent. So I invited this church friend out for coffee.

"I'd like to ask your forgiveness," I told her. "I should not have gotten so angry."

She forgave me right then and there and instantly—at a tiny table in a coffee shop, where a lot of forgiveness probably ends up happening. And then she told me in passing that she and her husband had met with Brent a while ago on a different matter, and during the conversation they had spoken to him about "your wife."

My heart sank and raced at the same time. A sinking, racing heart is a terrible thing.

"Oh, I didn't know that," I said to my friend. I felt myself grow warm, and not in a good way. I tried not to break into a crazy cackle sitting right there. I kept my face blank and my eyes friendly.

I was at another intersection, and this time I had to choose the right way to turn. This thing could have kept going on forever. It was time to stop. I thought about my husband. Brent had been gracious not to tell me about this complaint, and not to be annoyed that I had created a situation in which someone had used the term *your wife* with him—and not in the sentence "Your wife is so awesome."

I had arrived at this moment of apology with no pressure from him. I felt protected.

I went on to talk about other things with my friend that

day, our children and our town—safe topics where we could meet each other and start to rebuild.

"I love you," I said to my husband when I saw him later.

We are all messy and miraculous. Church scrapes us up against each other. It skins our knees. It wounds and then it heals. We are supposed to love each other all the time, and I don't think it ever stops being hard.

We are people with ragged edges. We are frayed.

But because we are in community with each other, pointed in the same general direction toward God—gathering, worshiping, praying, and eating at all those carb-filled potlucks—we help each other grow.

It would be better for me if growing in love and grace occurred while curled up in an armchair with a cup of tea (and a jelly donut) reading a book. But that is rare. We more often grow through failure and mishap, through shattered windows and things we should not have said. We stumble upon new levels of love because we have mucked things up or been mucked with by someone else, someone who acted wrongly or just annoyingly.

Often we grow because someone shows us something about ourselves that is ugly, and we need to turn away from that thing and move in a different direction, which is repentance. Church is ripe with opportunities for repentance, overflowing with prospects. It is possible to go to church to repent, then leave with even more to repent of.

Churches are filled with people. People are irritating.

Churches can be relied on for this, and also for special events, which often include a higher than usual concentration of the people who help us grow. Just the other day I heard a women's event advertised on a Christian radio station with the line, "Come and be freed from the spiritual bondage you didn't even know you had!" The announcer used a voice normally reserved for half-price cars moving so fast off the lot you had better come on down.

No wonder people think we are so stupid, I thought. Later I shared the story with a friend. I put my heart into it, mimicking the announcer's voice quite well, if I do say so myself. I had her doubled over with laughter—which I lapped up. And then we talked more about dumb stuff other people do.

When I read about the Pharisees in the Bible, I see myself in those stories. I rarely recognize myself in the heroes. At least not yet.

* * *

Once I was asked to serve as an extra driver for a women's church event and ended up with only one other woman in my van for the two-hour drive. My passenger talked quite a bit—almost the entire time, or so it felt to tired, grumpy me. "I know I'm talking a lot," she said. "I can't seem to stop." This did turn out to be true. Her stories were voluminous, but also sweet, which made me feel worse about feeling impatient. She told me the love story of her marriage, and the best way to make a macaroni casserole. I found it hard to concentrate. It was difficult for me to listen for that long, plus I knew I would never make my macaroni in the way she was describing, with canned tomatoes.

"The first service that one owes to others in the fellowship consists in listening to them. Just as love to God begins with listening to His Word, so the beginning of love for the brethren is learning to listen to them," wrote Dietrich Bonhoeffer in *Life Together*. Bonhoeffer calls this the "obligation of listening."

It is a ministry to listen to one another. And listening is the beginning of love. On my long drive of listening, I had not yet read Bonhoeffer's words. But something happened between the way there and the drive home that made my listening easier and kinder.

The day at this conference was miserable—for me at least. The icebreaker was a groaner and too long. The teaching was weak and colorless, I thought, like tea poured before it is steeped. Then we dispersed into different rooms where activities had been set up to help us relax and regroup and feel cared for, as women need. I chose the coloring room because I knew there would be a table and I could set out the books and journal I had brought with me and work on a writing assignment that was due to an editor soon. I certainly didn't want to waste my Saturday coloring.

I sat beside a woman who had a Bible with her, the same as one that had just been sent to me from a publisher who hoped I might mention it in the Christian magazine I work for. Writers and editors get sent this stuff sometimes. This was a Bible you can color. I hadn't dared, of course, because that would just be me wrecking the nice Bible.

But the woman next to me was the Monet of adult Christian coloring. She leafed through her Bible and held it up page by page for all of us to see her work. The women around the table gasped in admiration. Truly it *was* remarkable, but it was also a little strange to me, and because of my general unease with the whole day, the scene began to itch at me, as if I were allergic to everything and everyone in the room. I sank further into myself, dislocated from the women talking and visiting around me, and tried to write notes for my piece.

Then, *I am the smartest person here* floated through my mind, like a dark and horrible cloud. *Did I say that out loud?* I wondered with alarm, before I turned inward to tend to my bad heart. But the women kept coloring their pictures and gluing together bookmarks. The woman to my left kept showing her beautiful artistic creations. No one looked at me, horrified.

I closed my books and shut my writing journal. I rose from the coloring table, walked to the craft-supply table, and chose a picture to color—a very simple one with big flowers, roomy leaves, and a Scripture verse in the middle. Then I sat back down and turned to the woman on my right.

"Do you color often?" I asked.

"No," she said. "This is my first time."

She explained that her young daughter colored all the time, as girls of a certain age do—so seriously and attentively—and she thought it would be fun to show her daughter the picture when she got home. "Maybe she and I can color together now," she said. I agreed and told her how much I had loved to color with my daughter, Holly, so long ago, when she would let me.

I also discovered this woman was a minister's wife. She and her husband and three kids had moved from Zambia a few years before. Sometimes it was hard for her: Their church was small and her children were the only young ones, so it could be lonely. I listened.

Our coloring time drew to a close. I tucked my poorly colored picture into one of my books as a reminder that I am never the smartest person in any room—here, there, or anywhere—and that I had thought such an awful thing, which automatically disqualified me anyway.

My new friend and I walked back to the main room for more terrible singing.

Finally, mercifully, the day drew to a close, and it was time to drive home again. I resolved to listen better. I hadn't spent any time with my passenger since our arrival, so we caught up for a few moments about the day. I also asked her questions like "How do you make that macaroni again?" and "What do you like to read?" I volunteered my own stories that would fit into the flow of the conversation. I interrupted a bit, but kindly I think. I worked at it.

When we reached our church parking lot, where her husband was going to pick her up, he was there waiting. He smiled and waved, happy to see her. I wondered if he had found himself listless during the long day, wondering what to do without her. I thought he might have. "He told me he would make dinner tonight," she said as she climbed out of my van and into their truck. "See you at church!"

I saw her again the next Sunday. She told me her husband had cooked her hot dogs after that long, long day, and she shook her head and we both laughed. I caught a glimpse of her later in the church kitchen, arms deep in a soapy sink, cleaning up after the potluck. She's one of the women you can count on to always do the dishes or sweep the floor, or put up with the minister's wife.

Watching her, I felt like she had become someone I knew. And I knew I loved her, too, like a sister, like we are supposed to. I felt happy. I was moving closer, by an inch or so I think, to how God asks us to love each other. Maybe she loved me more now, too, her sullen, irritable driver who didn't even know how to make macaroni correctly.

This is theological. Church rubs us up against each other: my annoying self against your annoying self, grating sometimes and velvety smooth other times, so that we can learn to love each other as God loves us. And then we care for the world together. We know and we love—or we try to.

* * *

Once, on our way to the city, Brent and I went through the Coffee Time drive-thru on the edge of town. We ordered two coffees with milk from the woman who always says, "Thanks, hon," and "Here's your change, sweetie."

If she is not in a sweet-talking mood, Brent tries to prompt her sometimes with his own sweet talk, calling her sweetie, which I think is a bit silly. That day as we prepared to pay at the window, she said, "Oh, don't worry about that, hon. The car ahead of you bought your coffees."

This was my first brush with a coffee-shop random act of kindness. I was pleased, and my heart expanded—or so I thought. "Who do you think it was, Brent?" I asked.

By then a truck had pulled up behind us, and catching the spirit of the thing, I said, "We should pay for the car behind us." And I also said—quite clearly, I think—"But first ask how much their order is." He ignored that part.

"We'd like to pay for the order behind us," Brent said to the woman at the window.

We had to empty our wallets of all our cash because the order was so large. The guy in the truck must have thought we were rich and reckless. He had ordered coffee and donuts— maybe even lunch—for an entire crew of large men working at a construction site, or so I imagined. I was irritated with Brent for hours after that.

There are days when community gives very little and requires a lot.

Sometimes you are the one who needs the meals, the ear, the hug, the tender touch on the arm, the house cleaned, the kids watched, the shopping done. And sometimes—and maybe mostly—you are the one doing it. Church works best when we serve each other, and that is what we are supposed to do. Ann Voskamp, in *The Broken Way: A Daring Path into the Abundant Life,* describes giving as the antidote to fear and depression and isolation. "The real sinew of community, the muscle of *koinonia* [fellowship], is not in how well we impress each other," she writes, "but in how well we inconvenience ourselves for each other." It isn't having that makes us rich, she says; "it's giving. Give sacrificially, live richly."

I don't regret any single thing or thought or touch I have given away freely, but I regret the times I turned away, or turned inward, or turned back too late. When our beautiful friend Carys was dying of cancer, I couldn't think of what to do. And I was so busy. Then it occurred to me that I could read to her in her parents' living room, where she lay most of the time on a rented hospital bed. "Maybe The Chronicles of Narnia?" I offered. She said yes, but before I could find an hour during my packed, important days, she was in the hospital, in her final days.

It was fear and hesitation and busyness that kept my reading to her at bay and slowed my love down. I didn't tell her I loved her one last time, because I didn't show up on time. I was awkward in the face and fact of her dying. I didn't know what to say or do or how to be, and she looked so ill by then. And I allowed all that weight to bog me down. My love was there, but it poured too slowly, like ice-cold molasses.

In Steven Garber's book *Visions of Vocation: Common Grace for the Common Good,* he sets forth a way of doing and being in the world that applies to the planet and also to the parish. He says that once we know of a problem or a need and allow that knowledge into our hearts, we have an obligation to care and to respond. "And now knowing what we know, we are responsible, for love's sake, for the people and places that are ours—if we have eyes to see."

For years I judged my mother harshly for her deep sighs and for saying, "Just what I needed!" after a phone call about someone's grandmother dying, or about someone who was sick and needed help or a ride somewhere. Now I hear her weariness differently. My mother knew that it wasn't just a phone call with information; it was a pie to bake or a card to write or a funeral to attend, and I guess sometimes it was not convenient. It rarely is. But she responded. She said yes.

* * *

Once a year, we have an evening service at our church to mark Maundy Thursday, the night before Jesus died. It is one of the darkest and deepest services. Sad. We gather together—usually a very small group, because not everyone likes a downer church service—and remember that the night before he died, Jesus took bread, broke it, and said, "This is my body, broken for you." He took a cup of wine, shared it, and said that sipping from that goblet meant they were entering into a new covenant with him and with each other.

The Bible also says that Jesus stripped down to the bare minimum, wrapped a towel around his waist, got down on his knees, and did the work of a servant, washing the feet of his disciples and showing just what such a covenant meant— which is partly, at least, that to love is to serve. The disciples protested, but Jesus washed on, wiping and wringing out the cloth. He said that if they wanted to be his followers, then this was what his followers must do—love and serve one another by doing the exact kind of fleshy, smelly sort of thing he was doing for them. It was the doing and the pouring of love, and in the most basic and ordinary way.

During the Maundy Thursday service, one of the ministers washes other people's feet (without stripping to his skivvies, of course). He gets down on his knees and washes the feet of volunteers who are seated at the front of the church, facing the congregation for this public intimacy, this uncomfortable thing. Those who are watching crane their necks from their seats to witness the funny, odd ritual that has so little to do with our own culture but everything to do with how we are supposed to treat one another, live together, and point one another toward God.

One year, our two youngest kids were chosen to have their feet washed by the youth minister. They thought he was generally too bossy and ate too much of the pizza, and that his beard was too long. Holly would challenge his theology and request meetings with him to discuss what he taught in youth group. Poor guy. Ministers' kids are difficult to impress and impossible to fool, especially at youth group. They have seen behind the curtain. They live backstage. Pity the youth worker who has the minister's kids in the group.

When I told our oldest son—Erik, who had gone off to university—that Holly and Thomas had been selected for the foot washing that night, he said, "Oh no."

I'm certain our kids bothered the youth pastor just as

much as the youth pastor bothered them, but the thing about ministers' kids is they are almost always available for volunteer duties in the church because their dad or mom makes them say yes. So they get asked to do what other kids might get to say no to.

Sitting in the pew, watching them shuffle up front in the sandals they wore for easy foot access, I worried. They are wonderful and terrible, those two. They laugh at things and people, especially at church: odd singing, funny outfits, bad hair, big bellies, whatever. I was afraid they would blurt out something awful or look at each other as they might if they were alone—rolling their eyes, gesturing, forgetting they were in front of the whole church, barefoot and on so much display.

The youth pastor poured water from a ceramic pitcher into our family's popcorn bowl. When a big bowl is needed at the church, this is the one pressed into service. Holly and Thomas sat straight in their chairs, not looking at each other or the ground but toward the back of the church. For all I know, their dad was standing there shaking his fist at them. I didn't turn around to see. The beleaguered youth pastor knelt down in front of them and pulled the sandals off their feet one at a time, the same ticklish feet I used to kiss the bottoms of when they were babes.

He dunked their feet in turn into the bowl, lifted them out, and took a white cloth and gently wiped them down. Their feet were still and unmoving, cradled in his large hands. Neither of my kids laughed. They just watched as he dunked their feet into the warm water of the bowl and raised them out again. They allowed it. The youth pastor was tender and kind. He gently guided each cleansed foot down on the wooden floor beside the bowl, then gave it a little pat. Love commanded, given and received. Clean and dry.

CHAPTER 4

Marriage

Though one may be overpowered, two can defend themselves.
A cord of three strands is not quickly broken.

ECCLESIASTES 4:12

ONE MORNING when we were newly married and living in a basement apartment in Vancouver while Brent was in seminary, he held a small mirror above my sleeping face. I had been stirring, so he knew I'd wake up soon.

When I did open my heavy, sleepy eyes, I screamed. What I saw terrified me. My own naked, bare, startled face hovered above my own naked, bare, startled face. It was horrible. I did not expect to see myself, and never so closely or so clearly, and certainly not so early on a rainy day. I screamed and then cried, and later, after I recovered, I laughed. It's still the best trick my husband has ever played.

That's marriage. Your partner holds a mirror up, and you

must gaze at your barest, truest, most startled self, whether you like it or not. And this, too, is a bit of a trick. You may not expect this baring of every bit of you when you are standing that day at the front of the church, all eyes on you in that overwrought dress, exchanging the vows that lull like poetry but are so deep and terrifying.

You don't know then that you will be laid bare, for him and yourself to see.

*   *   *

We met in university in a seminar class called Latin American Dictators in the Novel, on the second floor of the arts building at Dalhousie University. The class read Gabriel García Márquez, of course, and Isabel Allende, and Alejo Carpentier's *Reasons of State*. On the first day, I took the last class outline and said, "Sorry." Brent laughed. I liked that. He popped up again in two of my other classes. I convinced him to attend a pub night, and I was so smitten that I told him I liked him that very same evening.

We dated. We would walk around campus together and write papers at the library, and I would kiss him in the elevator. He always asked me what my grade was on assignments before he would reveal his own. He was smart and funny and handsome, and good in a way that I had never encountered. He wore a scuffed-up green leather jacket and played the guitar— but he didn't know all the words to any songs, of course, because guitar players never seem to when you want them to.

We discussed everything. We argued about little and big

things, like whether it was good there was a law in Cuba that men had to do 50 percent of the housework and how to dismantle apartheid. Light and heavy. I had never met anyone so comfortable with his own opinions, and so I became more confident with mine. If he could say that, then I could say this. It was fun to debate in the dark dinge of the Seahorse Tavern.

Brent was religious. He read books about God along with his school assignments. He had a Bible open on his desk in his room. This was new to me, the way he talked about Jesus, alive and so real. I hadn't heard someone speak like that before. It intrigued me.

When I was growing up, my family had always gone to church; everyone on Windward Avenue did. I believed in God and Bethlehem and Easter. But Brent lived his faith in a way that I had not seen before. It made him not tell little white lies to get out of things, and he didn't buy lottery tickets. He was certain of heaven. His faith made him loyal and true. It made him show up on time and go to bed early on Saturday night and drive his friend Enrique, who didn't have a car, to church on Sunday morning. He called his parents regularly. He caroused less and pondered more. He gave away his kitchen table to a church that needed one, and talked with deep interest to taxi drivers and homeless people and little old ladies. I thought he was like a sexy monk.

He sang with that beautiful voice of his, and his faith moved him and made him believe in things unseen and invisible and mysterious but also simple and as clear as the stars in the sky. His faith helped my faith back then, and that is still true. Sometimes his faith is the boat in which I sit riding through the waves, knowing it will all be okay. This is one of the things he does for me as a husband and as a priest. He is as a home to me, and I hope I am a home for him.

*　*　*

We were married in a tiny Anglican chapel on campus because our own church met in a classroom in the dentistry building, and who wants to be married in a dentistry building? The pews ran down the side of the chapel and faced each other. Brent's relatives and mine sat on those hard, narrow seats, eyeing each other across the center aisle with its worn red carpet. Being a minister's wife was the last thing on my mind when I said "I do." The main thing was to be Brent's wife, and I could not have been more certain of that.

It surprised me the first time I opened my Mrs. mouth and my mother rolled out. I sounded just like the woman I had worked so hard not to be—because after all, that is what daughters do for a while. There Mom was, a mix of boldness and strange submission all at once. My mother had always seemed so capable, hosting fondue dinners and making fancy cakes after she took a course, although she read too many books during daytime hours according to my dad. At election time, she would turn to him and ask, "Now, who are we voting for?" And he would tell her. It occurs to me now that once she was alone behind the little cardboard partition, she might have voted for anyone at all. I hope she did.

I remember following Brent around an art gallery in

Tofino on Vancouver Island soon after we were married, picking up the statues he picked up, pausing in front of the paintings he paused in front of, looking at what he looked at, and moving on when he was done. I remember waiting until he had reached a conclusion about some event or meal or movie or, yes, politician before I made up my own mind, which was his mind, because that had been my mother's mind, which had been my father's mind. How awful and boring it must have been for him to have a parrot flapping around behind him. Or maybe it was nice.

In those first few years, I was caught up in what I thought it meant to be a Christian wife in a Christian marriage: We should be agreeable and no longer yell at each other about feminism and communism and consumerism and material- ism and all the other things we used to debate. Now we were married, and it felt like the debating should die down a bit, that we should be of one mind on things. His views on acid rain and the prime minister were less stimulating than they were before. Plus he required well-thought-out arguments from me, with sources and research, or at the very least good reasons for thinking what I did, and it got a little tiring.

I believed we needed to agree on at least some things. I read a magazine called *Virtue* back then, which my mother- in-law would give me, full of images of pretty women reading Scripture and baking in spotless kitchens. The way I under- stood it, they honored their husbands with their baking and with their agreement. I think that for a while I tried to be someone I was not—someone who agreed with everything her husband said and did and who waited patiently to find out what she thought about things. I was twenty-three, and it's easy for someone young to misunderstand what it means to be a Christian wife.

* * *

We were told to remember that we were marrying each other and not each other's families. I suppose that advice had to do with the cleaving part of the equation, that I was to become the most important and influential woman in Brent's life and Brent was to be the most important and influential man in mine. What we didn't know, and in hindsight would have been helpful to know, is that you may leave your families, but they don't necessarily leave you.

When I grew up, our basement was carpeted in red shag, from wall to wall and also up one entire wall. My dad collected beer mugs, and they were an important part of our decor, hung in the basement on wooden pegs. My sister, in her rug-hooking phase, painstakingly created art for our Canadian Mountie dad—that yarn image of an RCMP officer in his red serge uniform, standing at attention, also hung in the basement, reminding us of who our dad was.

My father commanded our adoration when he returned home from an event wearing his formal dress. He seemed even taller, even more handsome standing at our front door in that deep-red jacket with those shining buttons, his black pants tucked into those high brown boots. We loved when he dressed up.

There were poker nights for the men, when my sister, Miriam, and I were banned from the basement. There were potlucks and bridge games with groups of intense women sitting around a card table in the middle of our living room. My parents hosted RCMP parties featuring my mother's sweet-and-sour meatballs, served with toothpicks. A guest shoved the dining room table out of her way and danced in her heels in the dining room, scratching the hardwood. That story was told for years. My parents received an award for their parties, from an unofficial and secret award committee of the Mounties.

My mother sold makeup and carried it around in purple glamour cases, hosting shows in women's living rooms. The year she outsold everyone else, she was crowned the Glamour Queen. In a photograph from her coronation, she is young and slim and pleased with herself. She wears a small tiara and a purple satin cape trimmed in fake white fur. It suits her perfectly. She was beautiful back then, even though I didn't realize it at the time—because most kids cannot see that their mothers are so gorgeous. But I see it now. Her big sales year bought us our Coleman pop-up camper trailer, which changed our summers forever. All of us were excited but perhaps not as grateful as we might have been.

As teenagers, my sister and I were drinkers and dancers and butterflies, socially speaking. My parents didn't know where we were and what we were up to behind the school, but no one's parents did back then.

Brent and I came from different homes, which were on

different planets. Things matched in his. Broken and chipped dishes were discarded, not plunked back down into the cupboard. Dancing women who drank too much gin did not show up at their gatherings. There was encouragement to be logical and thorough and to perhaps make sense. They were less hysterical than my family.

In this new world I married into, I learned to send thank-you cards in a timely manner, gently reminded to do so by my mother-in-law, who once gave me a package of them, wrapped as a gift. I learned to pass bowls of caramelized carrots clockwise at family dinners, and to not begin dessert until the hostess finally, for the love of Pete, sat back down and picked up her spoon. When everyone was finished eating, the women would flow to the kitchen and the men to the den.

There are so many things that make us different from the person we marry. More than we can know or count. You enter marriage with all those habits and ways of doing things, and notions about what is fun and what is not and when to laugh and when not to, and the same with crying. You lug a past with you that you don't know you are carrying and opinions you don't even know you have—until you say them out loud. Your parents taught you things even when you didn't know you were learning, like how to say "I'm sorry" (or not) and "Please forgive me" (when you need to)—and why it matters so much.

The first and most abiding crisis, which began on day one, and now, on day 9,497 (approximately), still pulls us apart and then snaps us back together like an elastic band, is our deep differentness. As it has turned out, Brent and I are not two kittens warmly curled in the same little basket. To know this, and to know that it is okay to be different, has been a long and hard lesson, at least for me.

He has better taste. I am more fun, or so I say. He can sing. I can cook. He recites Monty Python—still. I hate that. I will knowingly wear socks that don't match and pretend, even to myself, that I don't realize it. He would rather stay home than do that.

He is neat. I am messy. For attention, I like to give him a rundown of all the housework I did so he knows something has been done. Then he says things like "That must feel good." And I must admit the awful truth and say, "Not really." I have to remind him to read a novel every now and then.

I don't have to like the same things he likes or want to do the same things he does, and I can go for a walk alone if he doesn't want to come. Sometimes he should just come, but he doesn't always have to. And I can pick the movie, and he can, too, sometimes.

It's okay that he doesn't want the stinky, shedding dog to lie on the rugs, even though I'd let Dewey sleep on the bed if I lived alone; but then Brent wouldn't be there, and that would be worse than the hardest things.

So we grow in our love of how different we are, and although it can be so, so annoying, it can also become a wonder. *Look how fearless he is to say whatever he thinks about anything,* I might think. And he might observe, *Look how gentle she is about what other people are feeling and thinking.* Over time, I become bolder, and he becomes more tender. And I can see that our togetherness is a way that God draws us closer to himself.

Marriage is not for everyone. But in my life, it has been a blazing and refining fire, helping me see myself more clearly and know where I need God's grace even more deeply.

* * *

The night of the Groundhog Day fight, we were getting ready to lead a marriage course at church. Brent and I were one of the mature couples who were hosting the series, which featured a DVD presentation followed by pleasant and reasonable discussions between pleasant, reasonable couples seated at small tables with candles, set up around the church hall.

"Your marriage must be perfect," one of the wives murmured to me as we waited for the evening to begin.

"Actually," I answered, "we just had a really big fight about Groundhog Day, so no, it's not."

She must have thought I was joking, because she laughed and laughed and said, "You are so funny."

It started at the dining room table when I told the kids the groundhog had popped his head up that day and seen his shadow, so winter would not end anytime soon. They peppered me with questions, excited about groundhogs and weather. And then Brent asked me something like, Why would we want to fill our kids' heads with stuff we know isn't true? And then I asked Brent something like, Why can't you just relax and have some fun, and who cares about the groundhog? And then he asked me something like, Why are you so flaky and silly, and what's next—aliens? And then I asked him something like, Why are you so boring and awful and terrible, and who cares so deeply about passing food in the right direction?

The babysitter showed up, and off we stormed the twenty feet that separated our house from the church, to host the evening about building strong marriages.

As it turns out, we can fight about anything. It is the *how* of the fight that really matters, not the *what*. But if you can take the fight by its clenched fist and lead it into the safety of your love, and into a room with the lights on, this is always better than silence and retreat or pretending to agree to get along.

It took us a long time to talk about the Groundhog Day fight without another fight. (We can also fight about fights.) It was a silly argument, but it exposed our differences, and marched them boldly in front of us. We didn't talk about it that night over candlelight in a church hall packed with other couples who went to our church and thought, for some reason, that we had it all together. But we did laugh about it a little later on, probably months and months.

* * *

"Ladies, enter his gates with thanksgiving and praise." That was the advice given in a marriage podcast about how to approach your husband with a suggestion or request, or a thought on how he could do something better.

For example, if I want Brent to get moving on fixing the doorbell that hasn't rung for months, I might first say, "I really appreciate how you take out the garbage every week," and then a few minutes later, "And so now I'm wondering about the doorbell." Or I might say, "You did a great job organizing the garage. You're so good at that." I'd wait a beat or two, then ask, "Hey, do you think you could pick up your clothes?"

This makes a great deal of sense, of course: To get anybody to do anything, just say nice stuff first. It was Brent who told me about this podcast series in the first place. He listened to it on long drives because he wanted to be a better husband, always learning. This touched and encouraged me. It made me want to listen to the podcast, too, so I could be a better wife. That was the problem—we both listened to it. So now if I say, "I just want to say that you are so smart and handsome and very, very capable . . ." he knows immediately what I am doing.

Before we married, we attended a weekly Bible study and potluck dinner every Friday night. It was run by a couple who would take a moment, if the opportunity presented itself, to teach us all a little something about Christian marriage. And the wife would take me out to lunch to share what she knew. I assumed, based on my dismal performance in the Bible Trivia game we played one horrible night, that she realized I was new to this business of serious Christian living, and probably a little lost.

One of those bits of advice she gave, offered over a delicious all-you-can-eat lunch at Pizza Hut, was to "build up your man." I remember the lunch vividly because we prayed before we ate. Now, of course, I pray before meals in restaurants all the time. It's second nature, although I do take care of it efficiently, because even after so many years sometimes I think about the people at the next table wondering what we are doing. But back then it felt like we had flashing lights on our heads and sirens going off at our table. Such a bare thing to do, to pray at Pizza Hut.

"Building up your man" means saying and doing things that remind your husband how much you love him, she told me. I tried this out on Brent and said something like "I love how you speak with such assurance," and he would say, "Oh, trying to build up your man, are you?" So, so difficult a person.

There are other prescriptions for a good marriage that Brent and I have both read, such as the power of the husband saying he is sorry. One book said this makes the wife melt. And the thing is, this does work very well for me. I may not melt, but I soften embarrassingly quickly, like butter left out on the counter—and we both know this. It's good advice, but it may not work magically the same for everybody, every time.

Something may work for one spouse but not the other. Saying that a certain shirt or pair of pants does not look good on your spouse is one of those things. If I mention this to Brent, he thanks me for telling him. He wants to know. If he says it to me, I am speechless. He should apologize; then maybe I could soften and we could move on. But he doesn't, because he's not actually sorry (and he's not a husband who can fake it), and this has now, for him, become about justice.

All of this points to the problem of marriage formulas. It's better if we just agree that we love God and each other and that he brought us together to stay together. We believe that our marriage and our home is a hospitable place for both of us, that we belong here and are each other's safest haven, and that this is the place where we love each other and reach out to love the world, which God has also asked us to do as individuals and as a couple. We help each other love better, even as we are each other's toughest projects.

When I think back now to that Bible study we were a part of so many years ago before we were married, I am sad. We all loved each other, and we had no idea the storms that would come. I knew even then that they worried about Brent and me and whether we would make it. We disagreed in front of them all the time, wrestling with anything that seemed too easy. We made things look too hard. We would have been voted least likely to become a clergy couple.

Our marriage is the only one that has lasted. The woman who took me out to lunch that day to offer me advice left her husband. A couple who met at the study are now long since divorced. Another man, whom I guess we didn't really know at all, committed sexual crimes and then committed suicide.

I don't know what any of this means. Maybe only that life and marriage are such hard work, and we don't all make it. Maybe it means that Doug, the quiet and kind minister who married us—and took us to a Paul Simon concert, which probably makes him the best pastor in the world to be married by—offered the best advice of all: "Treat your marriage like a third person," he said, "like a child."

It helps to think of our marriage as someone outside of ourselves who needs a sweater draped over her shoulders when she is cold. She requires us to check in on her, and she needs chocolate and water and champagne and our fiercest protection—and maybe even to be pushed high on a swing occasionally.

CHAPTER 5

Family

*Children are a heritage from the LORD, offspring a reward
from him. Like arrows in the hands of a warrior are children
born in one's youth. Blessed is the man whose quiver is full of
them. They will not be put to shame when they contend with
their opponents in court.*

PSALM 127:3-5

BEFORE WE HAD CHILDREN, there was Dave, our black Lab.
He was the graduation present Brent gave me when he finished his master of divinity degree.

Brent, rightly in my estimation, believed I deserved a gift
for "putting up with him," as he said. He gave me a thank-
you card in which he had written, "When we get to where
we are going, redeem this card for a puppy."

Dave, on his adorable puppy factor alone, almost did make
up for Brent and Ancient Hebrew. For months my husband
would lie in bed studying flash cards before drifting off into a
haunted sleep, muttering words I could not understand and
that he could never really remember. He told a woman in his

class to shut up because he had to try so hard to learn, and she was so chatty. She gave him the finger. It surprised them both.

A few weeks after Brent graduated, we were down on our knees in a breeder's backyard, selecting the tiny jet-black dog quivering alone in the back corner of the pen. We bypassed all the keeners squealing, "Me! Me!" and went for the shy, scared one.

"Don't give him any sticks to chew," the breeder warned us as we headed north, toward the forest.

We brought little Dave home to the small cabin where we lived that spring and summer, rented for us by the three churches Brent served in a summer ministry placement. We lived surrounded by boreal forest: crunchy with forbidden sticks, cut down the middle by an unused and overgrown airstrip.

"We think having a puppy is good practice for being parents," we told Art and Bertha, who hadn't asked. Bertha, or Bert, as we called her, was the matriarch of the largest congregation that Brent worked with that summer. Art was her husband, a handsome veteran with silver hair, a man's man who flew fighter jets in the Second World War and crafted us the most beautiful wooden bowl, smooth as butter.

There is always a woman in a church who gets things done. Bert was that woman.

"How about a shower in here?" Brent asked Bert, who hired a handyman to install it. This was so we didn't have to go to the houses of church members to bathe, which had been the original plan.

We requested a phone. Bert complied. One evening during a beautiful golden twilight on the prairie, that phone rang loudly through our little cabin. It was Bert, calling Brent from a community dinner to tell him there was no one there to say grace and ask if he would hop in his car and drive down and do it. They would delay the start of the meal, she said, until Brent could get there.

"No," said Brent. "You are perfectly capable of saying grace, Bert."

I listened with concern. I didn't want the woman who gets things done to be annoyed with us. But Art and Bert continued to extend grace to us. They fed and watered us like the summer transplants we were.

"Watch out for Dave when he's out on the airstrip," Art warned us. The caribou who milled around out there were mean and unpredictable, especially at dawn, especially in rutting season.

That summer, I did spend a lot of time on the airstrip with young Dave, wrestling sticks out of his mouth, training him every day because I didn't have much else to do, and nervously peering over my shoulder into the woods lining the neglected corridor of tall grass and tiny little wildflowers.

For a week or two, Brent and I ran a Vacation Bible School for the kids who were otherwise not doing much of anything, or so it seemed. We didn't have a clue how to engage with the rowdy children filling the community hall during their summer break, and they were not particularly interested in learning Bible stories, at least as told by us.

Brent preached three times each Sunday, at three different churches. He sped down highways and dirt service roads to barely make it on time to each one. We tucked Dave away in his dog crate in the morning, fussing over the blanket and ensuring he had a treat. By this point in the summer, Dave was beginning to lose just a tiny bit of his cute charm, no longer all long ears and warm round belly and now chewing up a lot of my shoes.

On those long, slow Sundays, the first time I heard Brent's sermon I thought it was fine; the second time I wasn't so sure; and by the third time, his sermon no longer made sense to me, and I dipped in and out of wakefulness, sitting alone on a pew, the sun pouring through the windows of the little wooden church as I thought about getting back home to my dog.

Years later, when we learned that Art had died and Bert lived alone in a seniors' home on the West Coast, we reminisced about that summer. We remembered how kind they were to us, a young couple who knew very little about anything. "I can't believe we told them that our dog was good practice for parenting," Brent said. "And I can't believe we thought it."

* * *

When we had our first child, the universe and all its mysteries snapped into place. I found the last piece of the puzzle I had been working on for a long time hiding under the table.

This was a great relief. It seemed that all my questions about what on earth I was here to do, all my wonderings about what God's will was for my life, were answered in this tiny person wrapped in a tiny blanket in that small, warm room. I was surprised at the ease with which a baby could hoist the whole world in the right direction.

It was a revelation to me how peaceful it felt, how correct and inevitable that this baby would rest in my arms and feel as soft and warm and solid as a heart, and in those sleepers. Erik's teddy bear pajamas moved me to tears.

I couldn't help but notice that other babies in the hospital nursery looked more like aliens or miniature old men with stern faces and furrowed brows, trying to solve big problems. *Just look at my baby, all round and smooth and sweet and baby-like.* I was comparing already.

I had no idea how complete my love would yet bloom. You really can't guess.

Finally, here was someone I would take a bullet for or jump in front of a car to save. In the throes of romantic love, I might have thought I would die for Brent. But if I were to die for him, then who would look after this baby, the one I was put on earth to look after? (I still fully expected Brent to die for me, especially now that I was the mother of his child.) I was thinking these kinds of things, lying in bed at the hospital, unwrapping gifts and having my back rubbed by the nurses and my food fetched.

It was a small hospital in a small town where everyone knew everyone else. There were a lot of Christians on the team, including my doctor and one of the nurses, another minister's wife. I wanted natural childbirth because I wanted to be fully present, and I guess I just love a painful challenge.

But I thought it was possible I would swear while giving birth.

I worried about this, almost more than anything else. What would our Christlike doctor think about the young pastor's wife as I roared out obscenities in the delivery room? I grew up in a culture rich with cussing; the people I knew well cussed extravagantly and creatively. They were masters. It was so deeply ingrained in me; who knew what I would say midlabor? It would be a death blow to Brent's ministry in this small town, I decided.

Like so many things I would go on to worry about, this, too, did not come to pass. I didn't know you can't speak, let alone swear. Both of our reputations remained intact.

We transported Erik home from the hospital, across the street to the rectory. Brent drove like he was ninety years old. The car crept slowly down the road, because who knew what traffic incident might be about to happen on Centre Street near the big cowboy statue. I sat in the back seat, where I would sit for years to come with one hand on the car seat, humming.

Brent prepared Dave for the new arrival by bringing home a blanket Erik had been wrapped in the night before (one of the many homemade baby quilts we'd received as gifts from ladies in the church) so Dave could be familiar with his baby smell. We had read how to do this, like we read how to do everything.

Dave resigned himself. Maybe now he could relax a bit since our focus had shifted from training him to be perfect to raising this little boy. Dave could chew as many sticks as he wanted, plus eat all the food sailing off the high chair.

With joy came fear. I had met some brokenhearted parents by then, and I was terrified of being wrecked by parenting. One thing about the church is that you meet people there who have seen some stuff and lost some people. There are such sad stories.

One couple in our church had lost their son in a car accident just a few years before Brent became their pastor. His picture hung in their house, their boy vitally alive, strong and young, a hockey player and a hunter, ready for the life he would not have. Nels and Dorothy had sad eyes. They were generous and heartbroken at the same time. When they held Erik and cooed over him, and when Nels fed him whipped cream from a tiny spoon—long before the suggested six-month eating plateau had been reached, as I noted later in my baby journal—it brought tears to my eyes knowing they had had a boy like this, a baby like that who had died on a road not far from their home.

When I was new at being a minister's wife, I wondered how people who had suffered such loss could hold on to their faith. Now I know that holding on is the way to survive. Jesus shows up in the horrible messes and the shocking sadness, and he does not leave.

My life was wrecked, I decided back then. Beautifully, forever wrecked. Because if you love someone this much, like you do your little baby sitting there in that tiny red T-shirt and a diaper, wearing those ridiculously small cowboy boots pulled over little yellow socks that won't stay on, then you have gone and done it. You have opened yourself to all the possibilities of a world that grows tulips but also has riptides—and Komodo dragons for some reason—and sinkholes and cancer and icy roads, where cars can skid out of control.

*   *   *

Before our kids were born and up through their younger years, if I met an adult who grew up as a pastor's kid, I asked questions.

"What did your parents do right?" I would ask. "What was it like to be a minister's kid?" *Tell me what to do and what not to do.* That was what I wanted to know.

Did they still attend church and love Jesus? Or had it all been destroyed for them by having a parent who was a pastor?

I almost always heard the same replies. If the church hurt their parents, those adult children carried that weight, and often anger. They felt protective of their parents in hindsight, angry at a congregation they felt betrayed them. I also heard from kids who felt they were second in importance to the church because their dads were always running away to emergencies, or taking calls at night, or not really being present even when they were with their families.

I tried to remember it all.

"My parents never spoke badly about the church in front of us," someone said. And I took that also into my heart. We vowed never to moan in front of our children. If there was a problem in the church that Brent wanted to share with me, he would do it late at night or early in the morning when it was just the two of us, with no child around to hear. We whispered. Kids hear everything.

I heard happy stories too. They knew they were special in the church. People paid attention to them. They remembered late-night Christmas Eve services and early-morning Easter liturgies that were the background music of their lives. They liked having busy houses with people coming and going. There was a hubbub of hospitality, and they remembered their parents praying and trying to do things right.

* * *

When Erik was three or so, I found him standing in the middle of our living room, frozen like a statue. His arms were stretched straight out on both sides. His legs were pressed together, feet straight forward. His head, with that gorgeous thick brown hair, was flopped fully down on one shoulder. Eyes closed, he stood cruciform and silent. I watched for a moment, waiting, but he didn't move.

"Erik! What are you doing?"

His eyes snapped open.

"Seeing what it feels like."

It was beautiful and tender, and to my knowledge no parenting book had any advice for this moment. His play was helping him to understand the pain of the world. Who hasn't wondered what Jesus' crucifixion felt like? I had stumbled upon a private moment of someone little trying to figure out something big. Sometimes to parent is to witness, and then to hug. So that is what I did. A delicious snack was also in order. And then I suggested that we go outside and play ball for a while.

He was a holy, earnest little fellow, following Brent's rule to remove his shoes so he wouldn't drag grass into the little tent Brent had set up in the backyard. If I saw him sometimes leave his shoes on, I thought, *Well, that's a relief.*

He would pray before our meals when we weren't in a hurry, thanking God for everything on the table. He was grateful for the ketchup, the salad dressing, the salt, the pepper, the fork, the pork. Through my semiclosed eyes, I would catch him glancing around to make sure he hadn't left anything or anyone out. He was a little priest, in charge of his small congregation.

I would answer his questions about electricity and the universe, just as he helped answer mine about who God was calling me to be.

*   *   *

Years later, our family was at a Chuck E. Cheese restaurant for Thomas's birthday. He had begged for years to have a birthday party at Chuck E. Cheese, where you can "make your child a star on their birthday." You choose a level—"star," "super star," or "mega super star"—which determines both how many tokens the birthday boy or girl (and their guests) receive for playing the loud, clanging games and whether a loot bag is included.

A giant mouse comes out and dances and carries on with your child and his celebratory gang, and you don't let your kid shy away from the mouse dance because you've paid all this money.

I felt embarrassed in front of our friend Peter. Peter was also a church minister, with the added weight of a PhD in theology. Peter and Tiffany's oldest son, Ben, was best friends with Thomas, our youngest son. This meant that Peter and Tiffany had not yet reached a stage in their life as parents and family where they would crumble and fall apart and finally agree to a pricey party at a loud food chain with a giant dancing mouse. I assumed their standards, and what they expected of themselves as parents, were still high.

Peter decided to stay for the whole party, as some parents do. He sat and observed at the end of the table, which was cluttered with empty pizza boxes, spilled cups, lost tokens, cheap prizes, and plasticware. I assumed he was thinking theologically about it all, about all the waste and silliness and running around and crying out for more candy—and that mouse. Peter seemed very mature. I felt fully surrendered to chaos.

This is a theme in my life as a parent: comparing our family to families who seem more together. This feeling of inadequacy—spiritually, materially, practically—grows like a weed in my garden.

There was a family in one of the churches Brent served that was musical and wonderful and good-looking. Every single one of them played an instrument, and the mom told me she prayed over each child as they left for school in the morning. Mornings were too hard at our house, and maybe that was because I did not pray. It felt like a miracle if we left the house on time, and then there was that long walk up the hill, pushing and pulling whoever lagged. I could not keep up with other families, and my kids could not keep up with me.

I felt a little ping in my gut when I heard of parents driving long hours for ski championships and hockey tournaments, and of kids playing in symphonies because they were so fabulously fabulous. We couldn't easily afford the lessons that made kids so amazing at things, and we were too busy already. We allowed them one big activity each. I worried that we were not doing enough; that I was not enough; that we were just stumbling from one parental blunder to another, depriving our potential geniuses and superstars of their shots at glory.

Our daughter, Holly, took ballet, as little girls do. When it was Halloween, their teacher, Miss Lynn, invited them to wear their costumes to class. Every other little girl was a fairy or a princess. Tiaras sparkled. Pink chiffon rustled. It was all delicate sweetness. Except for Holly.

She wore her elephant costume, thick and plush and gray and awesome—or so I thought until we went to ballet class and I sat on the other side of the oppressive viewing glass and watched her stomp around. The trunk hung heavy over her face. She couldn't see.

"Do you want me to tape up your trunk, honey?" I asked when they were having a little break from all their twirling.

"Yes, please!" she answered.

I borrowed packing tape and folded the trunk up and

attached it to the big gray head of my little girl, the class elephant. She could see, but it seemed even worse.

"Aren't you hot?" I asked.

"I'm fine. Just let me go," she said.

She moved slowly around the room in the circle with the other little girls, swaying to the music, distinctly herself—my sweet elephant.

Years later, drinking a pot of tea together, Holly told me this is one of her best stories. The memory is a treasure. She was an elephant in a room full of princesses, and she didn't mind at all.

I worried a lot—about what I did and did not do and about what my kids did and did not do. I was on high alert for anything that would make them feel deprived because they were minister's kids. I worried they might have enough reasons for naturally resenting the church without adding to that list things we could control.

The church—the sixth member of our family—is a weird and sometimes wonderful auntie. She can throw a tantrum or show up with an armful of gifts. She demands attention, but she also hugs you tight. She might reach over and give you a smack, right out of the blue. Sometimes Brent must rush to her side; it's his job. It is what he has been asked to do, and we are a part of it, too, just by loving him.

"What now?" I would ask Brent when the phone was ringing too much on his day off or on evenings he was home. I have tried to stop asking that. It does not help.

*   *   *

"Is your dad a nun?" That's what a young cashier asked Holly one night as they worked together at the local grocery store. "No, he's not," Holly answered, and we all laughed about it later and thought how strange it was that we were such a mystery to some people.

"Do you have to confess all your sins to your dad?" a classmate asked her that same year. I'm sure he must have been flirting, in a very odd way that never would have worked with Holly.

By the time our kids were in school, enough had changed in our culture to make ministers' kids seem perplexing and unusual—rare birds in a secular sky. I don't think people expected them to be perfect. I don't think they knew what to think about them at all. It is not so much expectations that can plague a minister's family these days; it is assumptions. People might assume your kids won't break a window or break a law or break your heart. But of course, they can do all those things and more.

In Sunday school, it was presumed our kids would know the answers to all those tough Bible questions. "You know, because your dad is the priest!" some kid would say, and probably he was right. Also, the teachers called on our kids more because the pastors' kids could be counted upon when called upon. Plus they were there every Sunday.

It's not that we studied the Bible at home more than any other family. I don't think we did. We had devout families in our churches. Some of them seemed far more capable of maintaining order during a suppertime devotional than we were. Over the years, our family would attempt different things, but inevitably, no matter how short and fun I tried to make those devotional times, we dissolved into laughter or tears or maybe yelling.

"If they ask a question," I would say to Brent, "maybe just try to keep the answer simple." It was difficult for him not to mention a theologian by name or some fact about the church fathers and explain how they had reached a certain theological position; or not to reference other Bible verses or maybe streams of themes from the Old Testament. He was a jazz player sitting at the end of the table, riffing and rolling and improvising, sometimes for too long.

Our young children's lives were drenched in church and faith. It was the ocean in which they swam. When we lived beside the church, they loved to run over to the office to deliver a message to their dad or play monkey in the middle on the church's front lawn with a giant pink ball we had bought at Walmart.

One day they fought all the way home from swimming lessons. We pulled into our driveway at the very moment Brent was leading a funeral procession into the church. "You will not say a word until that coffin enters that church, or there will be big trouble!" I threatened them. They sat silently in our van and waited, watching their father walk slowly behind the long wooden box, his white robes fluttering in the wind.

* * *

The messes and the misses are what Brent and I remember the most, what touch us so deeply—our clumsy selves just trying to do our best. There are so many real things that we did wrong, especially me with all my yelling.

I wish I had never once shouted. I also wish they had not stretched plastic wrap around the living room lamps as I watched, helpless, while interviewing someone on the phone for a magazine article I was writing about whether or not spanking was a good thing. I wished they had not dumped a can of beans in their brother's bed, or put all my bras in the freezer on April Fools' Day. I wished that a frog had not been dropped in a sink full of dishes because, as it turns out, frogs die in hot, soapy water.

I do love them well, and so deeply, and they love Brent and me well right back, even though sometimes they haven't liked us very much. They have shown me that this kind of love, so resilient and with so much room to breathe and stretch out your arms and stand on your toes and make mistakes, does not end. It does not snap back and become smaller. There is not a limit. It really is a faithful, heartbreaking, and heart-making love that is worth the feeling and the giving. It is worth the pain and the risk.

I see that now, even as I stand among them—all three of them taller than me now and still alive and well despite my worrying. I did not need to be so afraid.

There are things I wish I had done in the beautiful and even in the terrible moments. I wish I had prayed more often with them and for them. I wish I had pointed Jesus out to them more, especially when it seemed sometimes like he was standing right in front of us, and in the middle of us, and beside us. I wish I had trusted him more from the very beginning, believing that even if things would end up going terribly wrong, we would all still be okay eventually.

I also wish I had done those things I had planned to do, like cooking a meal from a different country every week, learning about the culture together (sitting quietly, taking turns reading out loud), and praying for the people who lived there (sitting quietly, taking turns praying out loud). I did not do that, not even on one single Wednesday evening. That was an idea I had before we had kids, something nice to do with your puppy maybe.

There may have been times when I should have put my hands gently on each side of Brent's face and said, "Over here," drawing him back into our embrace when he could not help but be distracted.

It is okay.

I will tell my children that if ever a young minister's wife asks them, "What was it like for you to be a minister's kid? What did your parents do right or wrong?" that they should tell the truth; the whole bruised and beautiful truth, so they can help her.

CHAPTER 6

Friendship

A friend loves at all times.
They are there to help when trouble comes.

PROVERBS 17:17, NIrv

BRENT AND I SAT at a table in a Chinese restaurant on a late August evening and said the names of our friends out loud over lemon chicken, ginger beef, and vegetable fried rice. We were seated on a patio overlooking a canal, where boaters navigated their way through the last days of summer. The heavens opened as they do sometimes, without warning, and everyone who had been standing at the water's edge dashed around. They were enjoying their evening watching the boats one minute, then running to search for cover the next. The rain beat down. We watched, safe and dry under our canopy.

I wondered what the people at the table so oddly close to ours had thought about our tête-à-tête, how desperate we might have sounded to them: two middle-aged people drinking glass after glass of water, trying to come up with a reasonably sized list of friends.

Our conversation occupied us the whole meal, from the minute the waitress said, "Enjoy!" and plunked down the platters of syrupy, neon-yellow chicken and the beef so sweet and crispy it sometimes appears in my dreams. Our exchange began because we had just spent two weeks alone on vacation, and maybe ended up feeling more alone than content by the end of it.

Our discussion didn't last so long because we had so many names but because we discovered we had so few. It was part list, part lament. Especially for Brent. I would say, "Well, what about so-and-so . . . ," tossing out names like Frisbees, hoping he would catch a few.

"Well, not really," he'd say, or "Maybe. I'll have to think about that one a bit more." It wasn't simple and straightforward because making good and true friends can be hard for everybody I guess, but especially, I think, when you are the minister or his wife. Your main community is your church, after all, and to the people in your church you are the pastor (and his wife), not necessarily someone at the top of their lists as the most fun guy to invite to a movie or golf.

There is also something that happens when you become ordained, a kind of veil that falls over people's eyes—the very fact of your career, the calling, becomes the way people see you. They view you through clergy-tinted glasses. You are pastors first, and often only. The witty guy who loves Springsteen and Alison Krauss and zombie movies and who had some other dreams for his life, too, may not have a chance to show his face very often. People don't ask questions about your life or your extended family or the types of music you love the most. They don't think to ask. You are mostly in their lives for a spiritual reason, and that does not include hearing about your hope to someday learn how to paint with oils.

They might not know what to do with you.

People in the church are trying to figure themselves out. They might be trying to understand who they are in relation to you, this person who takes Jesus so seriously and is pestering them to do the same, to take it all so deeply into every corner of their lives. That's your job, and sometimes it might annoy them. You are a reminder.

The pastor may hope to always be a reminder of grace, but that is wishful thinking. Sometimes the pastor reminds people of what they meant to do and who they meant to be, and the mistakes they make. The pastor might hope to always be a reminder of forgiveness, but he ends up being a picture of judgment, whether he wanted to be that or not. And the good ones never want that.

A pastor is probably in this work because he knows how deeply he himself has been forgiven. He has tasted this, as rich as honey, and so has his wife, or she couldn't possibly live through all those potlucks and meetings and nights home alone with the kids, or Christmas.

People just want to let their hair down sometimes, and there you are in the corner, all buttoned up tight, or so they assume.

If it's difficult to make friends in the church, it can be even more difficult to make friends outside of it, where most people think you are a weirdo. Your potential friendship list becomes very small, like your dog and his pals in the park maybe.

Old friendships may change too. When Brent went to his high school reunion, he was nervous to see all those friends after such a long time, knowing some would be shocked he was a minister. They knew him when he was a high school scoundrel and hadn't known much of anything about him after that. I'm sure the same would have been true for my old classmates too; they might have been amused and confused that I ended up being a minister's wife. They might have remembered me as a heavy smoker and a weekend drinker and the girl with the always-broken heart who barely passed chemistry—that is, if they remembered me at all.

This is when you become startling to people, a kind of wonderful proof that God does exist, and look what he can do with even you. You are better proof than an archaeological find from Old Testament days: You are there in the flesh, the same but importantly different. And years later, maybe these old friends will search you out and ask for help when they need it. That is good. They should. But you still might make them uncomfortable at a party.

* * *

It was January, and I was in New York City to attend the writing program I had enrolled in. Just outside the classroom there was a sign-up sheet for meeting one-on-one with an editor to pitch stories. I'm normally not aggressive about these things, having been schooled in the art of letting others pick out all the black jujubes from the bag first. But this time I shot out of the room and scribbled my name in one of the five coveted blank spots. Then I spent the next few hours trying to come up with my great idea, finally landing on one that had to do with my dog Dewey and how we visited senior citizens together. When my appointed time came and I made my pitch, the editor closed her eyes in boredom. Panic rose.

"What else can you write about?" she asked.

"I'm married to a minister," I told her. "I can write about that."

She perked up. I was an exotic flamingo, an uncommon find. I might have been her first-ever minister's wife. "Think about it and send me your ideas," she said. So I wrote an essay for her, which the magazine initially titled "The Friendless Life of a Minister's Wife." I asked if we could lighten things up a bit, and we compromised with "The Lonely Social Life of a Minister's Wife."

I wrote about how ministers can be misunderstood and how people assume you are both holy and deeply boring, but I concluded with a story about how our new next-door neighbors, Heather and Jeff, had invited us over for dinner even after they discovered Brent was a priest, and what a wonderful surprise that invitation had been, like a gift.

After the piece was accepted by the magazine, a fact-checker called—and asked for Heather and Jeff's phone number. I was accustomed to writing for more lackadaisical publications, so I was surprised by the thoroughness of the process. He wanted to verify they had actually invited us to dinner, even after discovering the sinister truth that Brent was a minister.

It took me a week to muster enough courage to call Heather. It was embarrassing admitting to her that because it was so unusual she had invited us oddballs for dinner, I had written about it for a magazine. But I explained the situation, and she agreed to verify my story with the fact-checker.

"Your neighbor might have the priest over for dinner again, but not his wife the writer!" said one funny friend.

I wondered then if Brent and I really were a double-negative whammy in the friendship world. "A priest and a writer walk into a bar" does sound like the first line of a not-very-funny joke.

Later I was recounting all this to my oldest friend, Janet, the cousin with whom I grew up sharing Christmas dinners, camping trips, and laughing fits. I explained how Brent and I are party wreckers. Janet found this hard to believe since I alone have the power to make her gasp for breath from laughing so hard. I asked her, "Well, if you and Dave were throwing a party, would you invite the pastor who lived down the road?"

She got it.

* * *

When we moved to Ottawa, we encountered for the very first time a ministry solely dedicated to the wellness of clergy families. They delivered a welcome basket filled with coffee mugs, crackers, and chocolates when we moved in, and I discovered they hosted an occasional study group for women married to ministry leaders. That is not to imply, of course, that there aren't men married to ministry leaders, or lots of women clergy. But this ministry recognized the challenges that women married to ministers might experience, and they attempted to create a safe space for them to study Scripture or a Christian book together. I signed up. At the first meeting, we were asked to share a little bit about ourselves and what we found wonderful or difficult about ministry life.

My answer was the same as always. My difficulty never changes.

"I find it very lonely," I said, "and it's tough to make friends." Most of the women around the table, which had a spread that included cheddar cheese, rice crackers, a little bowl of blackberries, and a jar of Nutella that appeared every week, nodded in agreement. They were lonely too.

In this group, I eventually heard a story about a minister's wife known for her friendship boundaries. When a woman from her congregation asked her out for coffee, this pastor's wife famously said, "We can have coffee. But I'm not going to be your friend."

I could not believe there was a woman so fearless as to say out loud what most of us have thought: *Yes, we can have coffee. But no, I can't be your friend.*

There are different theories about whether a minister and his wife can have friends in their congregation. I have had friendships that turned out badly, and others have turned out well—at least so far, so good. I am not an expert. Sometimes it works; sometimes it doesn't.

When it doesn't work, though, it really doesn't. I do know for certain that it is difficult—and ill-advised—to complain to someone in your church about your husband's loud snoring and fast driving and about how much he's on his phone. People talk. Your tiny story to share can become someone else's big story to tell.

But what if your husband, who is the pastor, really hurt you with that thing he said, and you are wondering who will help you sort it out? The best person is not Claudia, who organizes the women's breakfast at your church. This is because Claudia is also a broken vessel, and because of that, she might take some pleasure in hearing these things, and she might find it impossible not to share them with Sarah, who heads up the small-group ministries and is already annoyed with your husband. And soon enough the molehill will become a mountain that you will then have to climb.

It's also ill-advised to engage in gossip about other people, which we all know is wrong anyway; but it does happen. Yet it can never happen between a minister's wife and someone who attends the church. Even to be present in the room when talk like that occurs could damage your husband's ministry. It is just not worth it.

These are hard lessons to learn.

* * *

It is important to be transparent and real about who we are, all of us. But transparency is also a tender, fragile thing, carefully offered. It is transparency with limits and vulnerability with borders. This does not mean there is a cover-up; it means there is a tucking in of yourself. You do not give all of yourself away just because a good listener sits nearby in an armchair, ears perked.

This is the loneliness problem and the heart of the friendship mystery. "Our loneliness," said one of the leaders of my minister's-wife group, "is one of the sacrifices we offer up to the Lord." It helps me to view loneliness as an offering.

I read once, in an essay about loneliness in the lives of clergy, that in a crisis people in a church like to think of their priest or pastor as a holy person who has answers—and not as a wreck like them. Also, they might not like to make confessions, if they are required, to someone with whom they have fished for largemouth bass.

Who does the church need you to be? This is a true puzzle, a conundrum of the ministry life and a question that makes ministry life more difficult.

I have not figured this out, and maybe I never will. But when I meet a minister's wife who says her best friends are in her congregation, then I think I am meeting a minister's wife who hasn't slammed her hand in that car door yet. Maybe she never will. But if she does, I hope she will call me, because I would like to hold some ice on it until the swelling goes down, alternating with something warm, as doctors say to do.

* * *

When I went to see my daughter at camp, where she was a counselor for the summer, she told me that a volunteer nurse who came almost every year knew me from our university years. I couldn't imagine who it could be, plus Holly couldn't remember her name; so it was all hopeless—until suppertime.

I sat at what was known as the undesignated table, for volunteers and visitors—those who don't really belong at camp and aren't going to jump to their feet and dance to "Old Time Rock and Roll" to get everyone all pumped up whenever it plays. I made small talk with another visiting mom, saying my last name loudly and repeatedly so she could hear it over the din, and the nurse leaned into the conversation and said, "Stiller? Are you married to Brent?" We had found each other.

It had been twenty-eight years since I'd last seen Susan. She remembered that Brent often wore overalls, which I had forgotten; but she delivered the image back to my mind—how baggy and big they were under his jacket. I had liked them too. Her boyfriend back then, now her husband, had also gone on to become a minister, and it turned out they had moved to a city just a few hours' drive away from where we lived. After we had talked for a few minutes, we decided we should be friends—just like that, as if we were in a kindergarten classroom taking each other by the hand. This is because we knew we shared a semifriendless state that we could help one another with. A three-hour drive to their house for dinner? Easy.

I have had this experience with other ministers' wives, this petitioning of another grown woman I barely knew to see whether she would be my friend. I have had other ministers' wives audition me with a coffee date, and then at the end say,

"I need a friend." And I say, "I'm in!" Maybe we aren't alike in some ways, but we share some huge things in common: Our husbands are ministers; it's tough to make friends for all reasons good and bad; and the places where we spend so much of our time and energy, our church communities, may not actually be the very best places to find them.

*　*　*

Once at a dinner party, I kicked Brent under the table to get him to quiet down a bit. This never works. The topic was George W. Bush, which seems so minor now given where the world is today. For years we had been meeting with the same four couples every six months or so to have a potluck and maybe a fight. We even had a name for the group in honor of the slightly Indian-bent menu for most of our meals. We called it The Cardamom Club, and our kids snickered.

There we sat around a long table, two ministers' wives and two ministers' husbands with our spouses, yelling at each other about politics and theology or whatever. It was so much fun. There just aren't that many dinner parties where a minister can share any opinion at all without worrying how it will be heard and understood. We knew we could let it all hang out, whatever it was. We wouldn't offend anyone but each other, and that was okay to do. It was all preapproved. Permission granted.

I noticed this same dynamic once when Brent and I were invited to a dinner party where all the other couples were doctors or doctors' spouses. We were the only nondoctors there. There was shoptalk, but it was more than that. It was shoptalk on casual Friday, with no customers around. I can now confidently report that doctors don't like it when people show up in their offices with a list, or when they say they are so tired and cannot figure out why.

That's what our clergy dinner club was like; we could talk about anything, and we could speak in shorthand and be understood and not have to explain or apologize afterward. Even though Brent and I have moved away, we still listen to The Cardamom Club playlist Brent made with its 113 songs—the perfect soundtrack for a long-distance drive.

* * *

Years ago, when we left Saskatchewan, my friend Fawna, another minister's wife, gave me a beautiful teacup as a gift. Moving every few years can kick a friendship in the shins, but not with Fawna. The cup, which sits in my cupboard to this day, miraculously unbroken and not even chipped twenty years later, was meant to be a symbol of how we would still meet for tea—just over the phone. Back then, we talked for long chunks of time in her living room. We promised we were going to call each other regularly to keep laughing and talking and supporting each other, and I would drink my tea from that cup when we did.

We did not do that, not even once. But it didn't matter because our hearts were aligned. When we saw each other again years later, we could have said, "It's like no time has passed at all," except that we both looked quite a bit older, so we didn't lie to each other. It was still easy and simple to talk about big and little things. Our lives were so similar: Our devotion to our husbands was the same, and the work of our husbands and how hard it could sometimes be was the same; and that made us lean in across the table and take each other by the hand.

Our own work lives were rich and challenging, and we talked about that too. We made sure to ask each other questions about our careers that other people might not think to ask, so associated were we with our husbands' work.

One time Fawna and I were talking about moving and leaving parishes and how difficult that is, especially on the children. I asked her whom she kept in touch with from the small city in which I had first met her. She named a few people I could not remember, and then she said, "It's like I have a quiver on my back, and every time we move, I bring the friendships of a few people with me. They are the arrows I carry in my quiver." I like that.

* * *

Alison is an arrow I carry in my quiver. Brent and I met Alison and her husband, Kris, years ago in seminary. Kris studied theology for a year, and that's when we became friends. Twenty-five years of work and moving passed by, and then we found them again in our new city. My friend Facebook led me back to Alison. Our reconnection was instantaneous, beginning the day she showed up at our new house with soup—perfect since our furnace wasn't working.

We sat huddled at the dining room table, scarves wrapped around our necks, and she told me about her work and her children and the books she was reading.

She and Kris used to attend the church Brent pastored, though long before we came they had left to join another congregation—one that had a better youth program, which is often how these things go. For us, they were simply our friends, nothing more nor less.

Last summer, Alison and I frolicked together on a sandbar. I think we looked ridiculous, but we didn't care. The sandbar is almost right in the middle of Cold Lake, and it's a complete surprise. It rises throughout the summer as the water level sinks; then one day in August, it's suddenly a meandering mile long. You can walk it, run it, or crawl along it with an old friend.

We floated and then pulled ourselves along, moving together across the sandbar, with its warm and shallow water, as our husbands sat watching in a small aluminum motorboat beside a little island on one end of it. Brent held on to the branches of a leafy green bush to keep the boat from drifting away. They watched us as we stood up now and again and ran, splashing and laughing, clutching our middle-aged middles. I laughed louder than I had in a long time. It came from such a deep place inside that it hurt, which means it was good.

We wore sensible one-piece bathing suits designed to make things look better. There was something about the running-in-bathing-suits part of our sandbar time that felt extra freeing for me. I'm not a woman who walks around wearing only her bathing suit in front of company. I hide. I wrap myself up like a burrito.

There was a time when Brent and I lived in a very cold place, where many people had hot tubs, and parishioners would invite us for supper and tell us to bring our bathing suits so we could sit in the steaming water together afterward.

"No," I said to Brent when we were first invited. "I will not do that." I could not bring myself to reveal that much, to say to people in our church, after eating lasagna and garlic bread and flipping through their photo albums, "This is what I look like almost naked, just barely clothed. Let's crawl into that tub together!"

But this day at the lake, I was free. As we worked our way down the sandbar, I thought about how grateful I was to have Alison back in my life.

We talked about our work, our children, and the books we read. We talked about how beautiful it all was, and how smooth the sand felt and how tiny the pebbles were that every now and then broke up the sand's silky surface.

"I've always wanted to run a marathon," Alison told me, "because I'd like the experience of hearing friends cheering me on." Maybe it was the sun and the water and all the time we had on our hands that made her think of it on that day: "I think it would be so great to be cheered."

I can see how the cheering could be the best part of any marathon, along with someone handing you a bottle of water and telling you that you are awesome. But yes, especially the cheering. Friends should loudly cheer—and wave their arms too—when they see you come around the bend, continuing until you sail or stagger over the finish line.

Whether we come in fast or slow, we will all bend over and hold our knees at the end, catching our breath. "Well done, sweet friend!" we can say to each other until we hear those words much later, for the last and best time.

After a while, when we had reached the end of the sandbar, Alison and I returned to the boat and crawled back in. It was more like we were hauled out of the lake and dragged over the sides by our husbands. I suspect that part was horrible to watch.

"We must have looked ridiculous," I said to Brent, then laughed and caught my breath.

"You looked like mermaids," he said. "It was beautiful."

I believed him. And I don't always believe Brent when he tells me how much I remind him of a mermaid. But I think that with the sun and the water and the vast expanse of the lake and the laughter of old friends, he meant it. There are some days when it is especially nice to have loved one another for so long. And on that day, it was nice to be with a friend I had known for that long, floating together while Brent sat in a boat with his own friend, his hand grasping a berry bush that grew on a tiny island so our boat would not drift away.

CHAPTER 7

Funerals

....

Precious in the sight of the LORD is the death of His saints.

PSALM 116:15, NKJV

ASH WEDNESDAY KICKS OFF LENT. It's the opening act to a very long and sad concert. Lent, full of repentance and reflection, is the hard path we walk to Easter. Ash Wednesday follows Shrove Tuesday, celebrated around long tables in church basements covered with platters of pancakes, maple syrup, and as many sausages as you can eat: one last kick at the can of fun before Lent. The next evening everything dims—the lights and our spirits.

The Ash Wednesday service is mournful and quiet, so achingly beautiful, full of poetry and true things. "Create and make in us new and contrite hearts, that we, worthily lamenting our sins and acknowledging our wretchedness, may obtain of you, the God of all mercy, perfect remission and forgiveness . . ." We say things like these ancient words, read in unison from a prayer book.

It is cold outside and the church is dark and somber. Everything feels different. There is a request in the bulletin that we abstain from the usual preservice gabbing and be as silent as we can. There is always someone who can't manage it and yaks away like a chatterbox, oblivious.

"Have mercy upon me, O God, in your great goodness; according to the multitude of your mercies wipe away my offences. Wash me thoroughly from my wickedness and cleanse me from my sin," we read from the book of Psalms as the service gets underway.

The first time I managed to line up all three of our young and wobbly, sleepy children at the railing at the front of the church, their pastor-dad traced a smoky cross of ash on those soft, beloved foreheads, right on the spot where they usually received their kisses. The cross is a symbol of both knowing and belonging: We are known, and we know to whom we belong. We repent, and we receive.

And then their priest and father said to his very own children this awful truth: "Remember that you are dust, and to dust you shall return." Death will come to us all, and we parents pray it will come to us first, long before our children. Death does still sting, after all. But not forever: We know we will be raised again with Christ—that's the promise.

"Was it hard for you to mark our own children's foreheads

like that?" I asked Brent later in the brightness of our home as we watched the nightly news.

"No," he answered.

Pastors do hard and beautiful things all the time.

* * *

"Go to the funerals," we tell our kids. People notice you in their grief. They see you standing there. They feel you grip their hands tightly, and they glimpse you across the room, even when you're catching up with a friend at the reception, eating all the egg salad sandwiches. They are so glad you are there. You can miss the wedding, but you must not skip the funeral.

And sing. You must sing. Every funeral I have seen Brent lead, he has addressed this awkward issue. "Sing," he says from the front at the beginning of the service. "Sing the songs. The words are written in the bulletin. If you don't have a bulletin, put up your hand. This family needs you to sing." They need to see you, and they need to hear you. This is how they know they are not alone.

Funerals are also worship services of a sort. We are worshiping God even as we mourn and remember the people we loved, or maybe the people our good friends loved—because we want to be there for our friends. Their hearts may be torn open, not ours, but we feel the pain with them. We are saying out loud that we still believe God, even in this. We still love God, especially now. And we trust God's promises, or we try to. We are reminded and we are reminding others that our faith has so much to do with ashes and resurrection: "Earth to earth, ashes to ashes, dust to dust; in sure and certain hope of the resurrection to eternal life, through our Lord Jesus Christ; who shall change our perishable body, that it may be like his own glorious body, according to the mighty working of his Spirit, whereby he is able to subdue all things to himself." That's what the priest says somewhere near the end. Amen.

Sometime during the funeral, we will probably remember all the other funerals we have been to, because they are so similar, so sad and quiet. We might remember the first time death stormed our consciousness and broke our hearts, when it wasn't our pet rabbits or goldfish that had died—which, thankfully, are pretty easily substituted. We replaced Erik's fish, Aidan, behind his back several times with an imposter before we finally let the fish go for good and acknowledged that yes, this pet was dead. We buried Aidan with solemn ceremony in a matchbox in our backyard. Even those kinds of services teach us something about the once-here, now-gone-forever nature of death, this thing that was not meant to be.

Often our first big experience with death is a grandparent, and who can replace one of those? Their death may not be tragic exactly—a grandparent's death usually isn't. It's death's initiation, a taste of all the awful passings to come during life. Someone is gone who will not be replaced. No more bridge parties or housedresses or your nana serving you iceberg lettuce on a salad plate; no more visits on the couch telling her what's new—usually nothing—and answering her questions about school, as if she were the police and you were about to be swept off to jail. All of that is gone, and hardly anyone in the world notices—just this small group who are left and who loved her. And Death says, "You'd better get ready, because as bad as this is, things are only going to get worse where I'm concerned."

Death intrudes and shatters. It is a thief of what is good and beautiful and funny and wonderful and once in a lifetime and only once in this world, until things are made new again.

And so the funeral should be a promise to the family who are there in those terrible front rows, the worst reserved seating in the world. We promise to stand by them, to drop in, to call, to remember with them, especially when their sorrow is as huge as a country, like when they are grieving a child. But even when they're grieving a grandma.

At the funeral and in the days and weeks that follow, we have opportunities to say many, many stupid things. We must try hard not to. I have tried to stop saying things like "Well, she lived a good, long life" and "It's good she's out of her suffering." They might be true. They are not helpful. We don't need to say everything that is true, but everything we say does need to be true. True things that might be helpful could be "I'm so sorry" and "This is so hard" and "I don't know what to say" and "I love you."

Not speaking at all carries an important kind of truth as well. It is the truth of sitting and drinking tea and just listening, even when it's so uncomfortable, and after a while you would like the sad person to not be sad anymore and maybe snap out of it for a bit. Watching and walking with grief can make us impatient. But this is the ministry of presence, like the chaplains practice. Just be there. Stick it out. You don't have to rattle on. Just sit down on the couch beside them.

At a Bible study once, we were talking about death and heaven, and a kind woman with a beautiful heart said she tells parents who've lost a child that God must have needed another angel in heaven. She thinks this is helpful. I could see, looking around the table, that I was not the only person who wanted to plead with her to never say such a thing again. I didn't want to embarrass her, and it's not like I'm a heaven expert. Still, I'm certain this is a wrong thing to say, at every level of terribleness. When we're confronted with the great confusion of tragedy, we say dumb things that grow out of our clumsy guessing and our need to make sense out of what seems senseless. Just show up with some casseroles and clean their house for them, if they let you.

We know so little for certain. But I do know, for example, that when I was a child and the thunder would roll and crash in the sky and my mother would call out in her singsong voice that she guessed her dad was bowling in heaven with his friends, this was not the case. I am certain there is not bowling in heaven. And when a chickadee shows up unexpectedly outside the window of a friend, I don't think it's her cousin Ralph, who died two weeks ago, coming by to cheer her up. It's the people who wrap themselves around us like a blanket, then feed us, who offer the most comfort.

I also know Jesus called what comes after this "paradise" when he told the thief on the cross beside him they'd be there together on that day, a bit later in the afternoon. I know there will be a new heaven and a new earth because that is what the Bible says and what our faith teaches. And because I have heard enough beautiful stories about people who were dying saying things like "Yes" and "Let's go" and "I see you" and "Jesus," I believe the membrane that separates here from there is even thinner than we think.

* * *

For some reason, my Baptist grammy, my dad's mom, stopped attending church sometime in her eighties. Maybe it was too much work, or maybe the church had changed; she and my grampy just stopped going to Sunday morning service.

The church, though, did not stop attending to them, as it sometimes does. After they quit church, the pastor and his wife still came by to visit them and sit around their kitchen table and talk, sometimes for hours. This was discussed with awe and amusement within our wider family, partly because we did not experience our grandfather as a talker so much as a tall, silent man in a rocking chair with a big fat cat on his lap. But Grampy would famously chat with this pastor, then slide a twenty-dollar bill across the table and tell him he might as well go pick up Kentucky Fried Chicken for the four of them. This story about the visiting pastor and our talking grandfather made us appreciate them both a little more.

Grampy died first, and at the time it felt like too much

work for me to catch a plane and arrange some things and rearrange others so that I could attend the funeral. There are times in a parent's life when it feels like you are looking out over an entire arena full of children instead of just the three of them standing in the kitchen in front of you.

Dad told me it was okay not to come.

I should have gone. I regret only the funerals I do not attend, never the ones I do.

So when Grammy died years later at 101, I didn't think twice about attending her funeral. I had seen Grammy a couple of years earlier at her ninety-ninth birthday party, where she had placed soft hands on both sides of my face and said, "It's Karen." It might as well have been my heart she held so carefully.

The week after that visit with her, I launched a letter-writing campaign to Grammy. I would buy postcards whenever I traveled far from home, and I even bought local ones that showed geese in flight or RCMP officers standing at attention to remind her of my dad and her other son, who had also been a Mountie. I mailed them to the nursing home where she lived, on the long, winding river where the men of my family had fished from small boats in their spare time, and sometimes caught eels instead.

I mailed her an article I had cut from the newspaper about molasses and how it had come back into favor. I remembered her cookies and the smell of her house—warmth and dough-nuts served with precious maple syrup tapped from their own trees and measured out of mason jars.

In my notes I caught her up on family news, and when I asked a question of her, I would say something like "I wonder what you would think about this? Or that?" I did not expect answers, but I thought she might like to know that I wondered what she thought, and that I remembered her, as she had remembered me that day.

Then she died.

As it turned out, the Kentucky Fried Chicken pastor was back in town on a part-time ministry basis and able to conduct Grammy's funeral. This felt like a small miracle—grace in the grief. We met with him and his wife in the living room of the parsonage, another white house on the edge of a parking lot—a stone's throw from Grammy's grave, which was even then being dug for her burial.

We discovered the pastor and his wife had returned to the small town because although some things had gone very well in their new church, some things had not. There was a church-kitchen renovation project, and long-standing members of the congregation donated their fifty-year-old kitchen cupboards. The couple happened to be, providentially they must have believed, renovating the kitchen in their home at the same time.

"It wasn't me who decided we couldn't use those cupboards," the pastor explained. My heart sank. I knew where this story was going, and I turned toward his wife, who was sitting near me. I tried to tell her with my eyes that I felt her pain.

The couple happened to drive by the church and spotted the pastor carrying those old cupboards to the big blue garbage bin in the church parking lot—just to help out. They witnessed him hoist them up and over the side of the container. I imagine they stopped their car and watched him, or at least slowed down.

Poor, innocent pastor lamb. This is a ministry precipice moment, a cliff-edge kind of mistake that is almost impossible to back away from. In seminary they should devote an entire class to why you should never touch donated, rejected cupboards yourself. That's what other people are for, to say no to the old cupboards and the carpet remnants and the chipped dishes.

There was no recovery. So the pastor and his wife were back in the small town that had treasured them and called them beloved, and the pastor was able to do Grammy's funeral. He sang a solo of "It Is Well with My Soul," at my grandmother's request, with a passion that cemented him in our hearts. He also preached a gospel sermon, a call to salvation so clear that I could hear the shifting in the seats of Grammy's descendants, who were probably hoping he would wrap things up.

Last year, after my cousin's husband died suddenly, Gail asked Brent to do the funeral. He said yes, of course. I was nervous. What if he made my cousins shift in their seats?

Being a minister and being a minister's wife in the family are peculiar things—at least it has been for me and Brent. In the beginning, Brent could dampen fun family gatherings like a rain shower, just by showing up; people were trying to figure out this pastor in their midst and calculate how much fun they could still have in his presence. But he was needed when sorrow arrived. A minister might be the death of the party, after all, but he is the life of the funeral, the unofficial family chaplain called into action in times of need. He is theirs, and they are his true people, even if they are not his congregation. He is their church when they need one, and this has turned out to be part of Brent's calling. A minister will be asked to do the funerals of the cousins and aunts and uncles and sisters and brothers who do not have pastors of their own. He might be asked to do the weddings, too, but they are easier, clearer. There are white and gold balloons. They are festive and joyful, happy and hopeful.

As it turned out, my cousin's husband had a beautiful funeral service that day. Brent conducted it with the dignity and quiet control he always brings so that people know they are safe and held in his good, warm hands. He has an excellent deathside manner.

Later at the reception, held immediately afterward at the Italian hall just across the parking lot, a group of ladies circled Brent. Their own minister was a dud, they said, and they had snapped into full headhunting mode, trying to recruit him for their church. Their minister was probably home at that very moment, oblivious, maybe watching a football game and thinking he was having a little time off.

*　*　*

In Mexico, where Brent and I were vacationing when we heard that my brother-in-law Doug had died, there are underground systems of tunnels where deep pools of green water rest in natural sinkholes called *cenotes*. The pools seem bottomless and endless, and the water is cool and clear, fresh and beautiful. They call it sweet water. And that is what Doug was to my sister—sweet water.

This is what I said at Doug's funeral when I gave one of the eulogies. I had asked Miriam if I could speak because I wanted to honor Doug. He died in her arms at age fifty while they were shopping for a microwave at Berry's Furniture Plus.

Our vacation had ended by the time my mother's call got through to us. We were already booked to fly home that day. As soon as I got home, I dumped the vacation clothes out of my suitcase and onto my bed, sand scattering across the bedspread, and then filled it with funeral clothes and drove back to the airport a few hours later. My plane, departing before twilight, glided above the most beautiful golden clouds for most of the flight, and I pictured Doug standing on them, waving goodbye. I knew it was a silly, sentimental picture in my mind—the kind of image of heaven that makes Brent weary—but it made me stop crying for a few minutes and then start up again.

It had not been a simple, straightforward thing to welcome Doug into my sister's life or our family. Doug was her second husband, the man for whom she had left the first, and the first was a Jehovah's Witness. My sister had been part of that faith for twenty years and a leader in their local congregation. Just as I had jumped fully into my new life with Jesus years earlier, my sister had dived into her own life of faith, so different from mine. She was always fierce in whatever she did, whether she was ransacking my closet for clothes, defending me on the playground, or controlling the radio at all times; and her devotion to her faith was no different.

Everything changed for my family when Miriam became a Jehovah's Witness. She was still there, but not really. Present, but removed. When we did visit, conversations were often stilted and distant because neither of us felt we could talk about the most important things. Our devotion was so similar, but our theology was so different. My sister believed passionately, as I did, and she and her first husband raised their children that way as well, just as Brent and I were trying to do with our own kids.

Everything changed again for my family when my sister stopped being a Jehovah's Witness. She could not finish the race. Too many disappointments, too much sadness, and a marriage and a faith she could not save led Miriam to the comfort that was Doug. Her heart led her far, far away from where she had been. She divorced her husband and her religion, and in doing that, she lost contact with her adult children, which might turn out to be forever and is the saddest thing this aunty could ever write about.

When Brent met Doug for the first time, he was the minister meeting the man who had met my sister, who then left her husband and blew up her life, but who eventually seemed pretty happy, even with the sorrow of the loss of her children locked away in a compartment of her heart. Brent and Doug shook hands and helped my dad with the barbeque. The family chaplain had not been called to preach a sermon but to make a friend, and that's what he did. Then four years after Doug and Miriam married, he died.

By the time my flight landed and I made my way to my parents' house, my sister was asleep in a double bed in my parents' loft. She looked more alone than I had ever seen her, broken into pieces, the blanket tossed aside, as crumpled and wrecked as everything else. I crawled in next to her, which I had not done for years. We had been in a silly fight in recent weeks, bickering over something on Facebook, and that was barely mended. It didn't matter anymore. Small things wash away in the rain. I wrapped myself around her in that bed so she would know in her deep medicated sleep that she was not alone.

Brent flew in a couple of days later for the funeral. He and my sister went off together and spoke quietly in a corner, and I was glad. I knew he would know what to say and what not to say. He would know how to hear and how to just be with her. Family chaplain, here is your tiny congregation; brother, behold your sister.

We moved through those early funeral days like an army unit, with Miriam at the center. Our mission was to protect her from anything else that might go horribly wrong in her life, as if we could. We stood on guard for her, trying to make things easier.

Weeks passed. Grief rolled my sister up into a tight ball. She grew a shell. Our extended family, girl cousins especially, wrapped themselves around her like a quilt. Miriam moved into my parents' home, because she and Doug were building their dream house when he died, and it was not done yet. My dad finally built the closet my mother had asked him to build for years, and they hung up my sister's clothes. Even her shirts looked alone, with so much space between them.

There may have been a time in my parents' lives when they experienced impatience with those who grieved loud and long. That was long gone. They were deep in the trenches, the hospital, the hot volcano of grief. They were soldiers, doctors, rescuers. They were shelter. They fed and watered my sister for months; and eventually she told me they were driving her nuts. And I knew she would be okay.

In our extended family, Doug's death kicked off a flurry of blood work and updating of wills, even cemetery-plot buying. My dad called and told me he was about to purchase a family plot that had room for three and asked if I minded whether it was for him and Mom and my sister. How far we had all come to have such bald and bold conversations so often, almost every time we talked.

"Go ahead, Dad," I told him. I did feel a little left out, but I knew I would be buried next to Brent, near enough to my children for them to come with tulips when they wanted to.

After Doug's funeral, we gathered at his friend's house, and eventually we had a sing-along in the basement. Brent had borrowed a guitar and lined up with my uncles, my dad, and Erik to sing some Johnny Cash. I love Brent's voice, and I love when he plays, which isn't often enough. I know it touches a part of himself that he has stored away for another time—when there is more, different time. He played that night for hours.

The appreciative audience—me included—ate potato chips and listened to this group of beloved men who weren't half bad, singing and swaying together. It had been so long since I had seen Brent sweat not from work but from play, a parting gift from his friend Doug. I knew we needed more of that life, loud and cheering, while we are still here, while we still can, before what is next arrives so unexpectedly. Even if what is to come ends up being even more beautiful than we can ever imagine.

CHAPTER 8

Envy

Love is patient, love is kind. It does not envy,
it does not boast, it is not proud.

I CORINTHIANS 13:4

WE INVITED A COUPLE from one of our congregations to
our house, and they had barely sat down when the husband
looked around and said, "You have better stuff than we do."
His wife did not say anything, and it all felt awkward to me.

We did not have a lot of stuff, just starting out and all,
but we did have good stuff. Most of it was cast-off furniture
from Brent's parents, such as an elegant little set of teak side
tables from Indonesia you could stack together when you
didn't need them and cleverly pull apart when you did. We
had a smooth black leather chair with tiny brass studs circling
the back and seat that we placed under a heavy mirror with a
gold-painted frame, which Brent's parents had also given us.

Brent took a week to choose the correct wall and perfect height for hanging that mirror. Things were not hung higgledy-piggledy as in the house in which I grew up. Brent did not do slap and dash. This could drive a person crazy, especially my mother if she were visiting.

Still, he was usually right. Even the ugly wood paneling in our living room looked richer with the mirror hung just so and the black leather chair placed carefully under it and the side tables a finger-length away. The whole room sat up straight.

We also still had some wedding stuff—like the plates Brent's mother had herded us down to the department store to select, even though the very last thing I wanted back then was to choose a china pattern. I picked out the least precious-looking dishes available. My rebellion was to use this china every single day, not just for special occasions. We would eat our Cheerios from the expensive soup bowls because we were only going to own one set of dishes. The plates were thick—more pottery than the delicate fuss your mom took down from the china cabinet on Sundays; but they still looked fancy. Nothing had really broken yet or been worn down back then. We ourselves were barely used.

As for the guest who said that clumsy thing, weeks later I confirmed—silently—that our stuff really was better than theirs after they invited us to their house. We drove over through the snow, and when we arrived I was in full observation mode, even though Brent had cautioned me about this very thing. Brent and I had a bit of a history by then with my occasional indiscretions during long visits with people you really do have to listen to and you should want to listen to, not changing the topic or saying "Yes, yes, I get it," as you might occasionally say to someone who really loves you.

These official visitations could weigh me down. I was vulnerable to conversation fatigue, especially in small parlors while sitting on a floral couch. My eyes would glaze and my legs would twitch. "It's so obvious," Brent would say.

"Honestly, you don't have to come with me," he would often say. "Really, I prefer that you just stay home." So I finally did, reading books and maybe doing some writing.

Of course, a dinner party was something different, and that night, yes, I could see that our stuff was clearly better and, thanks to Brent's skill, certainly more beautifully positioned.

I wondered, though, why the man had noticed our stuff in the first place and why he had made that remark out loud once he had. Why did it matter? I have worried about our stuff ever since.

The house in which we had arranged our good stuff was called the rectory. The rectory came with a guy from the church, maybe named Gary or Frank, who was a retiree and popped by regularly without always calling first.

Gary or Frank was like your dad, if he was handy and made a few attempts to fix things himself before he called a real plumber. Our rectory sweated nicotine from the walls during hot showers, a problem no Gary in the world could solve because the previous minister and his wife and sister had all been smokers.

"It would be good to visit them," Brent said. "They're only a few hours away."

So we went to visit them in the apartment they now shared. It was a small, dim space. The lights were low, the curtains thick and dark. The snow on the side of the road that day was dirty, which does not help anybody feel good about anything. And the minister and his wife and sister were all very old and very smoky. I left that visit sad and a little panicky.

It is a fact that the old retired minister might not have minded his life in the least. Back then, when I was thirty, I often assumed people were either much happier than me or much unhappier than they probably actually were. "You always assume the worst," Brent would say to me. And it was true—I did.

I remember Victoria, a widow who broke my heart because she still lived in the same small house in the same small town where she had lived her whole life before her husband died. This felt like a failure to me because I knew everything. Then about an hour into our visit, she hauled out an oversize photo album jammed with pictures from the annual trips she had taken with some of her widow friends. "Here we are in Paris!" she said. Victoria had a squad. She chatted and laughed and pointed as we flipped through the photos. The stories flowed, and I felt silly; but I was relieved for Victoria.

So maybe the retired minister and his wife and sister were

also completely content, and I had jumped to conclusions because of the dim light and the worn furniture and the snow on that day. But after we had said goodbye to the old minister who was, I hoped, oblivious to my judgment, what I said out loud to Brent as we climbed down the apartment stairs into the biting winter air and, thank goodness, the sunlight was, "We are not ending up like that."

* * *

"I would make a very good rich person," I once said to Brent, by accident—because I should not have said it. I should not have said it because he likes to tell other people that story and have a good laugh. It's like his party trick.

I said it because by then I had been around so many people who, because they often had so much more than we did, bought name brands and seemed more carefree. We had people in our lives whose businesses had grown over the years in leaping leaps and bounding bounds, along with lots of old-money people who attended long-established churches. Being rich didn't look half bad. I wish I could say I hadn't noticed, but I did.

I thought I would make a good rich person because I would give so much of it away, and yes, also purchase copper-bottom pots and pans and hang them from a rack in my large, airy kitchen. I would invite people over for dinner all the time but perhaps order the food in more frequently. I would work less and volunteer more, benefiting just about everyone. That's what I thought.

Even just being a little better off than we were would have been okay too.

"What would be enough, do you think?" Brent, the wise sage, would ask.

When I was in university, I had a button pinned on my little bag from Guatemala that said, "There's no such thing as a rich Christian." I had bought it at The Red Herring, a Marxist bookstore downtown, which, needless to say, has long since gone out of business.

I had certainly moved a long way from that position. I could see how money straight in and straight out of the hands of the right people could do much good in the world, and I assumed I would be one of the good ones who just could not give enough away—while still dressing well and going to New York City for the weekend every now and then, of course.

Maybe the bad part was not my silly, fleeting thoughts but my envy. Envy grows easily in such dark, fertile soil. The more envy visits, the more easily it remains.

Another true thing is that you can envy lots of things.

You can envy someone's spiritual life. I envy the person who talks about the Lord as if he lives in that person's shirt pocket, hollering up instructions about what to do when and where. I envy the minister's wife who appears unruffled and does not charge into church at the last minute, who is always properly dressed and ironed.

Pastors can envy one another's churches. While Brent and

I were at a play one night, we ran into a pastor who had been a student along with Brent at the seminary he attended. We had not seen him for years. "How big is your church?" he asked.

I heard an author, one who writes beautifully and elegantly, speak of envy at a Christian writers' conference. A writers' conference is an envy conference, if we are completely honest. But there she was, a published author with a new book out, standing in front of a room of envious people, confessing her own envy. She spoke quietly, but I heard every word as she pulled envy out into the open. *I am not crazy or bad*, I thought. But I knew I still needed to work on it. Later, when I asked this author to sign the book she wrote (the one I envied), I thanked her for being so honest and helpful.

I told my friend I was with, who was also a writer (and blonde and gorgeous and able to speak softly and walk in heels, which I enviously noticed), that sometimes I envied her in a very general way, and also sometimes very specifically for the projects she got and the successes she had known. She said sometimes she envied me too. We hugged.

"Karen, bring it out into the light," Brent has said to me, and he is right.

There is a lot in the Bible, of course, about not envying, and there are a lot of stories about the problems that result when people leave their envy unacknowledged and unchecked, like a weed. Eventually it occurred to me that if envy is so frequently mentioned and so strongly advised against, it must be because it's so common. This was a revelation. When there are warnings, you can assume there might be a lot of people doing it. Envy is so everyday, like dust, and so boring and suffocating. It helps to know we are not alone.

Another thing that helps me, besides admitting my envy to God and having someone sitting beside me who treats me tenderly and is not interested in shaming me, is to behave in the opposite way that envy would seem to otherwise demand if envy were my evil overlord. Don't do what envy wants; do what love commands. This feels very biblical as well.

If I'm feeling greedy, it helps to be generous, even in a small way, like giving away a bar of beautifully wrapped apricot-scented soap I have been saving for a special occasion—to a woman I don't think I actually love but am trying to. It is a small thing, but a good thing. It also helps to pray for the person I envy—that they would have even more good things and opportunities, maybe another book published soon and successfully—and that they would flourish, which is such a good, rich word.

Envy grows in my scarcity.

It dies when I see my own plenty all around me, everywhere I look, and take conscious note of my abundance—and wish the same for others.

* * *

Once I met another minister's wife who owned a boat but had pretended not to. And as we all know, once you tell a silly lie about a sailboat, it's hard to dial things back.

Instead of saying, "Yes, that is our boat," when someone asked about it, the minister's wife panicked and made up a story about a relative who let them use it whenever they wanted.

I understood. I might have lied about the sailboat too. There is a temptation to pretend that you alone of all the people in your church do not own pretty things, or go to nice places sometimes, or occasionally buy new clothes, or go sailing on your very own boat—or that maybe you might like to, just like anybody else. I know other ministers and their wives who intentionally looked for houses that did not have curb appeal so that parishioners did not feel put off by their nice homes. I understand this.

Another minister's wife invited us over to her house for lunch one day shortly after Brent joined the staff of the large downtown church where her husband also served. This was a wonderful couple, older than we were, both of them highly educated, kind, and funny. They were interested in Brent and me and our lives. I loved them quickly. I was always looking for people to latch onto, to show me how to do this minister stuff.

"I love your house!" I said, when I stepped through the door. The furniture was solid and plush, and the light that streamed in through the windows brought the room to life. Beautiful paintings hung on the walls, and stacks of books looked read and loved, like friends just waiting for a visit. I felt at home right away because of how warm it all was.

Instead of saying, "Well, aren't you a sweetie?" which I think she might have been thinking, the minister's wife began to explain away their possessions, as if she had done this liturgy of distancing many times before. "That table is from a yard sale," she said. "That picture is not ours. I bought those dishes on sale."

She sounded just like me. "We have a friend who is an artist," I explain to people who wonder about one of our pictures. "That belonged to Brent's parents," I say to others when they ask about our side table.

I decided then and there, standing in my friend's restful room, that I was done with all that. No more explaining away my new sweater or telling the story of how we had paid fifty dollars a month for two years for a painting, because you can do that with hungry artists. I decided to try and relax a bit around our things, in whatever condition those things might be.

This is a hard thing.

Just the other day I agonized over the selection of new eyeglass frames in a shop in a mall, cheered on with a kind of raging optimism by John, an optician who used to be a carpenter.

"The only women who should wear men's frames are women with large noses," John explained when I asked about some of the men's frames I thought looked cool. Finally we had it narrowed down to two pairs. One of them had pink arms stamped with the name of their luxury designer. Brent languished in a chair off to the side, offering his opinion only when invited by John and me, but we both knew without saying it that if I bought the glasses with Prada printed on the side, I would spend the next few years explaining that I got them in a mall (I'd add "crummy mall" even though it really wasn't half bad) and saying, "They're not as expensive as you might think"—with a little hoot that would make me sound ridiculous. I'd probably add that I had just finished a big freelance writing job and that I wished those would come along more often.

It wasn't worth it. Plus I would get tired of the pink arms. So yes, if I had a sailboat, I would not know how to tell people about that.

Once we lived in a house that was too big and too beautiful. We bought it when we moved mid-school year, uprooting our youngest son, Thomas, in his junior year of high school. We wanted him to attend a high school with a rugby team, which he loved to play. The real estate choices were slim, either this lovely house that was too big or that lovely house that was too small. We chose too big, and I never did get used to it. The kitchen had recently been renovated and had a huge island with beautiful lights hanging over it. You could not slam the cupboard doors if you tried; they sank slowly back into place with a sigh, like they were happy with themselves.

"I do not belong in this kitchen," I said.

"It's not *that* nice!" my mother said, trying to make me feel better.

I was a house imposter. It was a good house for hospitality, though, with a dining room large enough for our table, leaves all in, and a living room large enough for our meetings. But I worried that it was too nice and that it made some people in our church uncomfortable, and that made me uncomfortable.

I did get used to the kitchen, however, because it's easy to get used to good, spacious, and shiny things. But Brent and I both wanted to downsize quickly after Thomas graduated from high school.

We are all just trying to figure out this stuff about our stuff.

I do remember that Jesus advises us to store up for ourselves treasures in heaven, not on earth. I do know that my heart will follow my treasure; or in some cases, my heart will follow other people's treasures. That is envy. I know Jesus said we cannot serve two masters. It is God or money. We choose one. If we choose the wrong one, our souls will be sick and thick and sad. And my battles with envy have convinced me of this truth even more. Even though it's uncomfortable, it is helpful to me that our faith requires us to not be so attached to stuff; that we are commanded not to covet, including our neighbor's donkey, if they have one.

This is something to continually work toward. We are not to covet—or hoard either, I would imagine. That includes clinging, which applies to my collection of identical antique bowls of different shades that I have collected over the years from secondhand stores; and to my beloved books; and to the painting of the zany woman with a cat, watering her flowerpots, that Brent found at a yard sale in Saskatoon one Saturday morning.

"Look at the birds of the air," says our King Jesus. "They

do not sow or reap or store away in barns, and yet your heavenly Father feeds them." So let's worry less. It will be all right.

I do watch the birds and their simple, spacious lives in the branches of the big tree in my small backyard, and I marvel at how free they seem to be and how their nests can be small and full at the same time. I try to worry less about all we have and all we do not have. And I suppose I can understand why someone might prefer that their minister have an old, dented car and a smaller house than they themselves might live in, and maybe worse stuff overall. And this is why a minister's wife might explain that her nice thing came from a yard sale or her mother-in-law's basement.

The world we live in approves of all our longing and our envy. It cups its hands around the little flame of our envy and blows it into full life, if we let it. Gratitude, though, smothers envy and discontent, like a thick blanket thrown over that small fire.

"Thank you," I say out loud to God as a discipline and a declaration, and in saying it I enact it. "I trust you," I say, and by saying it out loud, I recall from deep within that I do, even as I pledge that I will. I remember I am grateful and decide to be grateful again, right then and there in whatever very small or very large room I happen to be.

I know Jesus is always happy to hear this from a minister's wife, or anyone at all.

CHAPTER 9

Prayer

Then you will call on me and come and pray to me,
and I will listen to you.

JEREMIAH 29:12

LATE ONE NIGHT, Holly and I drove down dark, deserted Highway 12 on the way back from the train station. She had been in the city all day. It was the kind of late-night pickup that all mothers do, in pajama pants and sweatshirts.

We rounded a bend in the road and entered a confusing landscape of twisted metal and broken glass. A crushed car faced the wrong way on the road ahead of us. Smoke hung in the air.

I steered our van to the shoulder of the road. Glass crunched under our wheels. *Who would leave such a mess behind?* I wondered. I realized it was an accident that must have just happened.

"Holly," I said, "we are the first people here."

My immediate thought was for ourselves, how if we had been five minutes sooner we might have been part of this tangle of metal and crunch of glass.

"Stay by my side," I said as we climbed out of our van and I called 911. Holly quickly ran around the van to join me. I was acutely aware of my daughter beside me, seventeen then, and I was already thinking how this would be especially awful for her, so young. It's funny how we think of ourselves so automatically.

I described to the woman on the phone what I saw in front of me: a car severely damaged, a truck on its side a little farther down the road. "Thank you, thank you," I said over and over to her, because for a few moments it felt like Holly and I were the only people left alive in all the world, along with this woman and her comforting voice.

"There is glass everywhere," I said.

Other cars arrived then, solid and lit up, safe and intact. Other voices filled the air.

"He is gone," a woman called out from beside the wrecked car.

It was Holly who said we should go over to the car to see whether there was anything we could do. I hesitated, wanting to shield her. But she took my hand and led me across the road.

"Be careful, Mom," she said, pointing out glass and metal as we approached the woman who had called out. I knew her—it was Danielle, and she attended the Pentecostal church in town. I used to write local stories for her husband, who had been editor of the small-town paper.

The young man inside the car looked vulnerable, as if he were newly born instead of just gone. I felt a rush of grief for him, and I thought of his mother, whoever she was.

Danielle is a nurse accustomed to the hubbub of an emergency room and being around people no longer alive. She reached deep into the car and pulled a cell phone out of the man's pants pocket. "Here, see if you can find out who he is," she said as she handed me the phone. It was locked—his password and identity a mystery.

"Maybe we should pray," Danielle said. We reached for each other's hands, and standing in our small straight line, we asked God to help. We prayed out loud for this man and asked God to somehow comfort the people who loved him. We prayed for his mom and dad, whose hearts would break soon, their lives splitting in two halves: the before and the after of this accident they did not yet know about.

It felt like we had been brought together—the three of us—for this very reason: to pray for his family at this moment.

We prayed, taking turns, until a tow truck driver arrived, burly and red-flannelled. He swore at us and asked what we thought we were doing. He seemed angry, as if our prayers were a trespass to him and not intercession. I think he was trying to protect the young man from us, as if our prayers might harm and not help.

"Let's go, Holly," I said. Prayer awakened me, and the

tow truck driver's reaction startled me. The paramedics had arrived. I was aware of the lights, the crowds, the noise, and my desire to get Holly out of this mess.

Why was he so angry? I wondered. Maybe the tow truck guy was one of those people who think faith is a naive, made-up story and that car accidents in which beloved young men die prove that God is not real.

But tragedy reveals God to us, if we can just see him there in the mess. It is bewildering, but it is not empty of God. It is full of God, actually. It is when most of us feel God is most present and closer to the world than usual, like a gauzy, floating curtain blown off a window by a strong and cold wind. Just for a moment you can see more clearly through it.

Brent's college roommate used to say that faith was a crutch, as if that were an insult and proof that it wasn't real. Young in years and new in faith, I was offended. "It is not a crutch," I probably insisted back—outraged—then handed him some theological book I thought would convince him that God is real and faith is good, a book he would most likely never read.

These days I see crutches everywhere I look. Everyone hobbles, leans, and lurches, feeling their way gingerly forward. My crutch is real, solid beside me.

When my sister's husband, Doug, died, our father aged before our eyes. He seemed more fragile, bent over in a way I had never seen in this tall, strong man. The protector of our family realized he could not protect his girls from everything.

Just after Doug's death and before the funeral service, during that in-between time that is so thick with grief, my father stood in his living room and shook his fist at the pine-log ceiling he had built, a shelter for his family. He shook his fist at God and tried not to cry.

"I know," I said.

The fist shake did not deny belief—it declared it: *I know you are there. And I am so angry.*

We are bewildered in the midst of tragedy, and we should be. We stand huddled together in these giant freezing rainstorms of our lives, holding each other up. And we pray, especially late at night when we are standing next to an accident, witnesses on the side of the road.

The sadness of the accident haunted us. Brent called local funeral homes and discovered who the young man was. Holly and I wrote a letter to his parents and told them we had been the first to arrive at the accident and that we had prayed for their son, who we now knew had been in his midtwenties.

"We were there. We saw him. He was not alone for long. We prayed for him and for you. We prayed that God would welcome your son into his Kingdom and that you would sense God's love and comfort." We said we hoped they wouldn't find the praying strange—that we believed in Jesus and loved and trusted him, so we had brought their son before this God we trust.

We wanted the parents to know that two mothers and a daughter had watched over their son for as long as we could.

We told them about Danielle the nurse and how she had found their son's phone safely stowed away deep in his pocket, in case they had wondered. "We have boys too," I said. "We would want to know they were not alone and that someone had prayed, if such a thing were to happen to our family."

Holly and I also explained that we were a minister's family. I'm not even sure now why we included this part, but I guess we hoped it might help in some way for them to know.

And then we wondered whether the letter was selfish and worried it might bring more pain. Moments like this are when I trust Brent the pastor.

"No," he said. "This is a good thing."

On our way to do Christmas shopping downtown, we stopped at the funeral home, and Brent carried our note inside, in its crisp white envelope. He asked the staff to give it to the family whenever they arrived to make their arrangements.

With the letter gone, we felt a slight lifting of the heaviness we had been carrying, as if we each had taken off a heavy backpack and dropped it at the back door.

We were embarrassed to even be thinking about this weight of relief when we were alive and shopping downtown.

* * *

We are invited to pray all the time, about anything and everything. Peter reminds us in one of his New Testament letters to "cast all your anxiety on [God] because he cares for you." Most of the New Testament is made up of letters—some which you'd want to receive, others not so much.

Peter is the disciple who denied he knew Jesus when Jesus was arrested and beaten to within an inch of his life. Like most betrayals, this one of Peter's seems tiny at first, just a few words: "No, I'm not with him, not one of them," he said to a girl who noticed him sitting by a fire in the courtyard. But there are always two betrayals—one against the other person and one against ourselves. Sometimes our idea of who we are and what we are capable of stretches beyond recognition. I know this.

I like Peter. He is the disciple of choice for people who enjoy big, bearded men who might have crumbs down their shirt and say awkward things at dinner parties. When Peter first responded to Jesus' call, he was sometimes frightened and frail in his belief. Yet after his resurrection, Jesus came back and offered Peter a chance to say he was sorry—and Peter did, a few times in a few ways.

I can fit there, where losers can be leaders, where betray-ers can be restored and teach us to cast our anxieties and worries, our traumas, our everythings onto God because he cares for us.

I try to do this. I try this casting all the time when I remember to, especially when things are going badly or when I think they're about to take that turn. I try to cast my work, my children, my marriage, and all our family's best-laid plans onto the God who says he cares.

I remember the moment our youngest son, Thomas, was born not breathing, silent and soft. I waited, panting on the bed. "Please God, please God, please God," I prayed, dialing the heavenly 911 over and over again in my heart. He revived. I hope I said thank you immediately, but sometimes we forget.

In many of the psalms David wrote, he cried out for help, accused God, and begged; he said exactly what he was thinking—the whole kaleidoscope of every weird thing a person can think about himself and others, including ugly thoughts about his enemies. The Psalms are poetry, raw and real. Almost each one follows its own mini story arc, often beginning at loss and despair, swinging down into anger, and then landing somewhere new and relieved at the end. They say things like "I cry out by day, but you do not answer, by night, but I find no rest."

I pray like that too. I say things like "Where are you?" and "Why is this happening?" I fold my hands and shake my fists.

There was a time when what I prayed the most was "I trust you." I was forcing myself to say something out loud that I didn't really feel. We had just moved from a city I liked to a town I didn't, and I longed to be content. I would say, "I trust you" out loud into the air several times a day because I wanted to be that person—someone full of trust. I also wanted to be sure we were in the right place, that there was a plan for us, and that we hadn't wandered over into someone else's story by mistake. Whenever I prayed, I wanted my feelings to catch up to my words, which they eventually did. But it took a while. And I suppose I wanted to remind Jesus that I was trying.

It is difficult to pray in the raw and be brutal in our

honesty, but it is better. Somehow we don't think that we can be who we really are when we pray; we think we need to clean ourselves up.

We seek, and we hide.

Sometimes when Brent and I are at someone's house for dinner and they pray before the meal, I suspect they might be praying mostly because the pastor is there, because everything changes. It goes quiet and serious and awkward as the last dish thumps onto the table. No one knows what is about to happen, or not happen, in those few seconds of awkwardness.

My extended family does this sometimes, growing stiff and suggesting we pray, using words they wouldn't otherwise, such as *thy* and *if you so desire*. They become superpolite, less sweary, and more somber when they pray, turning red and not quite knowing when to stop.

Somehow we make them feel they need to pray in front of us as if they were praying to Her Majesty, the Queen—by way of Shakespeare. We tell people to pray if they usually do, but they don't have to just because we, the prayer police, are present. Usually, though, people seem to want to. It's an opportunity to pray, having the minister around. And I guess that is beautiful.

But prayer is not a test we can fail. Prayer is talking to God—and listening—in a simple way that we need not complicate. It's mysterious enough already. Pretending in prayer is a waste of time and a waste of love.

These days, if I fall into envy and wish that someone else's new car was mine or that at the very least my own car did not have crumpled mail on the floor and muddy dog paw prints on the seats, I admit to God that I have this feeling. I name it and hand it over, fighting the urge to pretend I never thought that, or felt this. I confess my annoyance over the nicest people who trap me in the grocery store by the sweet potatoes. This is such a relief.

Stanley Hauerwas, a theology professor at Duke Divinity School, published a book called *Prayers Plainly Spoken*. His prayers include lines like "Thank you, God, for giving us ordinary lives" and "Weird Lord, you never promised us a rose garden, but right now we could use a few daisies or zinnias." Hauerwas writes, "God does not want us to come to the altar different from how we live the rest of our lives. Therefore I do not try to be pious or to use pious language in my prayers. I try to speak plainly, yet I hope with some eloquence, since nothing is more eloquent than simplicity." Thank you, Stanley.

*   *   *

At the sale table in a theological-college bookstore, I found a deeply discounted prayer journal. It was a spiral notebook with blank lines under a heading like "My Prayers," and on the very next page an equally abundant number of lines for "Answered Prayers."

If only it were that simple.

Our church prayed for years that our beautiful friend Carys would be healed from her cancer. We gathered in groups around her. We prayed alone in our homes and when we drove and when we walked our dogs. We prayed at Bible studies and Sunday services and special prayer gatherings on snowy nights and over Facebook. We prayed by her bedside when she was moved to her living room so her parents could tend to her more easily, and we prayed in the hospital—even on the last day. We cried out to Jesus to save this darling who could enchant with her voice and her orange guitar, this woman who loved him so much.

Carys died and a thousand hearts broke.

Prayer is painful mystery. In every church we have attended, there have been women praying for the same thing over and over, faithful to their hearts' desires and dogged in their persistence. Almost always these pleas have to do with wayward children who have hurt themselves or their mothers and fathers, and often the prayers have to do with their children's faith. These mothers want their children to know the peace they have, the love they feel from God.

Sometimes the women, reaching the end of their prayer ropes, ask out loud why in the world wouldn't Jesus grant this one simple thing: to restore the faith of their children—a thing that enhances his own reputation. They don't understand why they don't get an answer.

Sometimes they might ask for my opinion, but I don't understand it either. And sometimes they ask me to pray for their family problems, or their aunts, or their pain. I want to explain that I don't have a special line or connection, that they are probably better at praying than I am, and that I might forget. I don't say the part about forgetting out loud. But I did learn from a friend that if someone asks you to pray for them, it's best to do it then and there. I try to do this—over the phone, in the church parking lot, wherever.

We pray and we ask; sometimes we receive, and sometimes all we get is the assurance that everything will be okay—but maybe not until the very last page.

Once when Brent was a seminary student, I went to a movie with another student's wife. As we pulled into the packed parking lot, she said, "Let's pray for a spot close to the door."

"Okay!" I chirped, because I wanted to seem just as trusting as she was in her belief that God, the Creator of the universe who surely was busy in Africa with more pressing matters (or should have been), cared where we parked at the theater.

She prayed out loud for a good parking spot. I said amen. And we got a spot, right next to the door.

I do not understand this.

Maybe God was feeling expansive that day at the movies, shuffling cars and movie times and schedules around to make space near the theater door for our convenience. Or maybe he said yes to my friend to teach me a lesson since I felt so uncomfortable. I pretended to go along because of my impostor tendencies, but I did think she had more faith than me—because she dared to ask.

Years later, here I am, still trying to figure that little thing out—and almost always walking from the far corners of parking lots.

*   *   *

Brent and I usually have a weekly Bible study in our home. I sometimes dread it on its scheduled day, longing to collapse in front of the TV instead. Dinner is rushed. I clean and tidy the areas in the house that someone might walk through or glance at. But when people wander in around 7:00, I am happy they are there to puzzle out life together and share how the week has been, to read Scripture or a book that helps explain it.

On one occasion, Brent was away. Brent is like the pope of any Bible study group we host. When he explains things, people believe him—or pretend to. All any minister has to say is something like "Well, in the original Greek, the verb tense would indicate otherwise," and debate withers and people get up to go to the bathroom.

That night, one of the men, seated on the yellow couch in our living room, cleared his throat and started to talk about prayer. My mom would have prayed, "God save us," because this man was holding court just a little bit. "When we pray," he said, "we should just thank God ahead of time for answering our prayers. This shows him we believe him."

The idea was that God likes it when we demonstrate such confidence; it shows we trust him. We might say, "Thank you, God, for how you will heal Betty" or "Thank you, God, for how you're going to provide me with work" or "Thank you, God, for the financial blessings that are yet to come (but are so close I can almost smell the money)."

I am more comfortable with thanking God for what is clearly already on offer to us, things like love and forgiveness, mercy and new beginnings; things that are for sure and safe and not so risky. I told the man that I had never heard of praying like this, but I'd try it because I'm always looking for the next great thing. And I mean, why not?

So I tried—and it felt like cheating. "Thank you, God, for enabling me to make more money. Thank you for how our kid, and you know which one I mean, is going to do his homework and clean up his act in general. Thank you, God, for how this church will grow." I felt silly. I thought Jesus knew exactly what I was up to, trying to sneak things in the back door. I abandoned that approach almost immediately.

These days I just try to be honest, as much as I can and as often as I am able. My prayers are saying less and less instead of more and more. If I pray, "I trust you" or "Hello" or "I'm saying yes but I feel like saying no," it is the best way for me. Saying the name of the child keeping me up at night with fear and worry is lifting that child straight up to God, without me explaining and telling God what I think is best. I might just bring their names to God like an offering and ask him to please protect them.

There was a worship song that I listened to over and over again with the refrain, "It's yours, all of it." I sang that out loud, and loudly, when I was by myself, and I saw the faces of my children, all three. I liked to think I was singing them into safety and myself into trust. I prayed as I sang and sang as I prayed.

God can see what is wrong and needs to be fixed, as well

as what is best left alone for now. I think this might show more faith, not less.

In her book *Sacred Rhythms: Arranging Our Lives for Spiritual Transformation*, Ruth Haley Barton encourages us to imagine Jesus asking what we most want from him. There's precedent for this in the Bible when Jesus famously asked a man begging for help, "What do you want me to do for you?"

Barton says to believe Jesus is asking you this question, too, and when you have your answer, to distill it down to as few words as possible "until you have a prayer of about six to eight syllables that flows smoothly when spoken aloud and captures the core of your deep yearning for wholeness and well-being in Christ." She calls it a breath prayer.

Your prayer can also be a phrase from Scripture. Often, my breath prayer has been "Please take care of me" or "Help me love you more" or maybe "Show me where you are, pretty please." Sometimes, and more often lately, it's just "Thank you." I've been trying to do this simple, short kind of praying more—when I'm walking the dog, or sitting in my favorite armchair, in my rising up and going to bed—and the begging-for-stuff praying less.

* * *

Six months after the young man died in the car crash, his parents wanted to meet Holly and me. They had emailed us a response to our letter when they first received it, saying they might want to see us in person someday. That day had arrived.

Holly had special plans with friends that night, and I encouraged her to keep them. Ministers' kids see a lot of crying—maybe too much. They have been to so many funerals. I wanted Holly to go and have fun. I made sure Brent would be there though. I was scared to be alone with people who were in such grief. It intimidated me.

When the young man's parents arrived, I opened the door to find them standing at the top of the stairs, each holding a bouquet of flowers. I started to cry almost immediately, seeing them in front of me—this mom and dad we had imagined and continued to pray for, these parents living with such loss.

They sat in our living room and told us about their son—what he liked to do, that he was lighthearted, and how he and his younger brother had been so close. They believed he fell asleep at the wheel while coming home from a shift he wasn't supposed to be working.

His mother leaned forward in her chair and asked me to tell them everything. I knew she needed as much as I could give her, and I felt we had entered into a sacred mother pact. So I offered up everything, every tiny detail I could conjure up, just as I would have wanted for myself. I told her how strange the scene had felt when we first arrived and about calling 911. I told her about Danielle and how surprised we had been to come upon someone else we knew—and how right it had felt to pray. I described the paramedics arriving and how they had worked on her son. I told her we had thought of them so often in these last months. Time had dashed by in a blur for us, but I was sure that for them those months had crawled past on torn and bleeding knees.

We were all crying by then. The young man's dad asked for a tissue, which usually I wouldn't have had on hand because I've always thought of tissues as a luxury. (Why pay for Kleenex with all these rolls of toilet paper around?) But I had just bought some from Trader Joe's while on a work trip because I could not resist the quips printed on the box: "I'm there when you need to pick up icky things" and "I'm there when you're sad." I handed him the whole silly box. Crying and laughing rub up against each other all the time. Life and death share the same space.

They told us that the minister who officiated at the funeral had read the letter we wrote to them out loud at the service. It helped them and other people, they told us, to know their son had been covered in prayer that night. "To think," said the dad, "that someone like you would be the first ones on the scene."

He meant a minister's wife and daughter and a Pentecostal nurse, women who believed in the holy and could give care to his son in a way that others might not think to. This was not the time to remind him that we, too, were full of questions and doubt and mess and muck. It did not matter. And we had brought some kind of offering that night: We prayed. We had obeyed a holy nudge and said our clumsy prayers. I saw that our belief and the very fact of our prayers had comforted him.

When they left, I prayed again: "Thank you."

Holly kept the tulips they had brought her in a vase in her room until they dropped their petals, like tulips do with just a glance in their direction or the lightest brush of air moving past.

CHAPTER 10

Disappointment

If you harbor bitter envy and selfish ambition in your hearts,
do not boast about it or deny the truth.

JAMES 3:14

I SAT IN THE FRONT SEAT of a SuperShuttle from the airport, baking like a bun in my long black winter coat. The sun is tricky in Newark and toasted me and my fellow passengers through the windows on that frigid January day as we drove into New York City.

"What do visitors do in Canada?" asked a tourist from Miami who shared the bus with me. *Big, whole, gigantic, sprawling Canada?* I offered a brief overview of the oceans on either end, the mountains, the prairies, the Maritimes, and Toronto. I added Montreal at the last moment to make us sound better. "What is the population of Canada?" he asked.

Ha ha, I laughed, then said, "Actually, I'm not sure."

Neither of us could believe it. "You're kidding me, right?" he said.

And that was the end of that.

I was there as a writer taking a course, and I had brought with me one big suitcase and some pretty recent minister's-wife baggage.

We passed a giant David Bowie mural, building-size. It was Bowie as Ziggy Stardust. I wondered if this was new, painted since he died. It had tiny lights on top to illuminate its crazy bright colors. My temperature continued to rise. I didn't want to mess with my zipper, which kept breaking like a small child's because I still hadn't remembered to get it fixed.

All of that—not knowing Canada had more than 36 million people, my stupid zipper, feeling like a sizzling sausage in my straitjacket of a coat, plus David Bowie's gigantic face—struck me as almost unbearable. And there it was again—the disappointment in my mouth—that even though we had come within a whisper of it, we would never ever live in New York City.

* * *

The pastoral position Brent applied for seemed like the perfect fit for my perfect idea of the rest of what would be our nearly perfect lives. Brent had spotted the ad on the alumni page of the seminary he'd attended.

"Why not?" we said. "You never know!" We were adventurers, after all; risk-takers, we thought. From where we lived in a small town, applying for a job in New York City was applying for a job on Mars. So far-fetched—until it wasn't.

Brent navigated several rounds of interviews, always moving on to the next stage. We had knocked on a very big door. It swung open, and it seemed like we were moving step-by-step up the deeply carpeted staircase on the other side; it led to the penthouse apartment of ministry life, at least for me. The idea of moving to New York City began to grow in my mind until there was room for little else. Ambition seized me by the heart and would not let go. My want became a living thing. It bloomed and spread and puffed up like bread rising in a warm place, barely hidden by a tea towel.

Brent was excited, too, but in a more realistic, grown-up way that mostly had to do with the challenge of the work. He did not get as worked up as I did, imagining the pot of geraniums I would place on the stoop of the brownstone that in my mind had already been rented, or the lovely stems purchased from my pretend friend at the corner store, whom I could perfectly imagine. I mentally tagged all the stuff we wouldn't take—the burned pans, the old furniture. We would start a new, hip life for new, hip us. I would be the coolest wife of the coolest pastor, and I would be a writer in New York City.

We flew down for a weekend of lunches and brunches. On the first day I leaned over the railing of the High Line park walkway and chatted with a church member who was giving us a tour. We discussed how Brent and I might transition our kids to big-city life. Then there were more interviews with

Brent alone. I walked to Times Square. I loved the lights and action, although I wished the people dressed as Elmo and Hello Kitty could have at least kept their fake furry heads on when little kids were around.

We stayed in a boutique hotel with dim lighting, dark and moody. Brent walked into closed elevator doors because they were so black and glossy and the light so dim. "We need to pull it together," I said.

Then he preached on Sunday morning. Audition sermons should be humble and bold; funny and serious; insightful but not too clever; well researched but not academic; on the shorter side but still weighty and meaty, easy to digest; memorable but not annoyingly so. I shot Brent encouraging looks as he preached. He nailed it.

We have sermon-listening history, he and I. I've had to work on "not bulging my eyeballs out" if I think he's gone too far or too long. Rolling your eyes is discouraged, and having a fight right before church, or even on Saturday night, is a horrible idea. Also, laughing at the funny parts in the sermon is good, but don't laugh too hard or too loud. Being the loudest to laugh is fine at a dinner party, but maybe not in church. Brent had performed the theological acrobatics of gathering all the Bible readings for that Sunday—the Old Testament, the New, and even the psalm—into one riveting message. I think it was about trust.

During the coffee hour I mixed and mingled, working the room. Then we went out for Thai with a handful of church members; they asked questions about our lives and our kids' interests, and a bit about my writing. I appreciated their questions. Typically church people aren't so interested in what I do for a living. They see me as the minister's wife, and that's usually enough for them.

"If you come, can I call you Father?" one young university student asked Brent. Brent said, "Yes, of course, if you want to." The student smiled and thumped him on the arm.

We flew home beginning to believe this might be the next thing God had in store for us—shimmering, shining New York City.

Glee bubbled up inside me. I smiled to myself as I walked my big dog through our little town—walking on air mostly, imagining the gasps of surprise, the widened eyes, the teary goodbyes. We would be generous hosts, offering a free place to stay in New York. I imagined people imagining us there. *People will envy us*, I thought. I was sure of it, and I found myself liking that thought. People don't often envy ministers' wives. They are more likely to say things like "I just couldn't do it. I could never be a minister's wife."

Weeks passed. "Nothing yet," Brent would say when I would email or call him at work to ask if he had heard anything.

Then five weeks after we had been in New York, Brent called me from a study break to tell me he had not gotten the job. He read me the email—*We like you, we thank you, we wish you all the best in the future.* I was already crying before he finished, a collapsed helium balloon. Brent was philosophical.

"Tell me you are disappointed!" I wailed to him on the phone. I didn't want him to have it all together so quickly and to immediately be so accepting and so faithful. I wanted him to join me in agony, at least during this phone call.

"I am disappointed," he said, "but it's going to be okay. They must have the right person for the job, and it isn't me."

He called again later. "Are you still crying?" he asked, amazed. I should never have pictured the geraniums on the brownstone stoop.

I had thought Jesus was giving this move to me especially, because maybe I was a favorite and he was finally realizing it. I had started to believe that I deserved New York City.

I was embarrassed, even in front of myself. I felt tricked. Why all those positive signs? Why had he not stopped us in our tracks before we had traveled so far down this road? Why watch my want stretch so large? I had thought this job and move was a giant bouquet of delicate orchids delivered to my front door—a thank-you gift from God for all the times I hadn't said "Please stop talking to me" on a Sunday morning; for the cities we hadn't lived in; for the money we hadn't made in some other job; for all the neighbors we'd never gotten to know because they thought we were from Planet No-Fun-For-Anyone.

Meanwhile, all over the world refugees fled, and people died. Friends lost jobs. My disappointment seemed petty and small compared to the bigger problems of a world that limped. Christians were being persecuted more than ever according to the statistics that flowed down my Facebook feed, and I thought I *deserved* New York City? I added shame to my stew of dismay. I felt bad about feeling so bad.

I knew I had to shove my way through this. It was not going to be a quick recovery. I had made room in my life for my big want; now I had to make room for my big disappointment. I looked at it closely. I asked it questions. I took it with me on my walks with my dog, my feet now firmly planted on the hard ground.

The holy, messy Psalms reminded me that I stood in a long line of disappointed pilgrims. I wasn't the first to be kidnapped by ambition and thrown into the trunk of a car.

One day on a walk, I finally admitted to God, "I thought New York City was our reward." I had entered into my own liturgy of lament, and I was going to see it through till the end.

And as if I were in a conversation in the middle of the silent road, I heard, *I am your reward.*

And I said back, "You are not enough."

It was my confession, and it shocked me. I shocked myself. But it was what I really felt in the deepest part of myself, and I had to express it. I said the worst thing I thought I could say to the God who loves me, and I was not struck down, but lifted up. My admission cleared the air and started the slow process of clearing my heart.

The day was still gray and cold. The dog sniffed and scratched at the dying beige grass on the side of the road. Nothing got better right away, but I had taken the first step.

Think anything and say anything. God can handle the truth. Of course God can.

I saw a man on the other side of the road nailing orange siding onto his house. It seemed remarkable to me. The house was tiny, on a small lot between larger homes. Hardly noticeable before, it was transforming into brightness, plank by plank. His action seemed daring and joyful to me. He was changing things with an attitude and siding, a kind of defiance of all the beige around him. I bet his neighbors hated it.

"I like your orange house!" I called out. Dewey danced at my feet, anxious to move on. The man didn't hear me.

"I like the orange!" I hollered again. "Thank you," he said, and picked up another bright board.

Years ago, when we moved to the only place I had said that I did not want to live, I was amazed that the bishop who said yes to Brent lived in that very place. I wondered why I had ever opened my big mouth.

I hadn't known then about the hardy friendships that grow from prairie soil. I didn't know how trees can be gifts, or how alive flax and canola look when they grow purple and yellow, shoulder to shoulder in neighboring fields like girls in bright party dresses. I didn't know that pelicans lived there, like the biggest surprise, on a quiet, deep lake in the north.

I hadn't yet birthed babies in hospitals where nurses offered massages and husbands could sneak back late with congratulatory pizza. You might see your doctor in the soup aisle at the grocery store later that week, where he would ask how you were feeling.

I hadn't yet canned whole baskets of ripe red tomatoes in my very own kitchen, and with my very own hands, tapping on the silver lids to confirm a good seal.

I trust you.

I am trying to trust you.

Thank you.

I am trying to be thankful.

I began to pray for the people who had gotten the job in New York. I asked God to bless them, especially the wife. I prayed they would do well, that their preparations for the move would go smoothly. I made myself imagine their excitement. I asked God to protect them and help them. *Bless them, Father.*

This was a hard thing to do. It helped me.

Saying thank you to Jesus for all the wonderful things happening to people you envy draws out the infection. It is your mother's cool hand on your blazing forehead and her voice saying, "Come here, sweetie." It is an unusual comfort. It is the bath towel she would warm in the dryer for when you stepped out of the tub and into the cool air.

Of course, you choose to pray like this—it won't come naturally. You might not actually want to do it, ever. But if you do, you can heal. *Bless their work, their move, their job, their new lives. Keep them safe. Nourish them. Make them even more well in their being. Help me to stop being such a jerk.*

This all helped.

Darlene's name came into my mind one morning, like a mercy. I hadn't talked to her for years, but as I sipped my morning tea, I knew she could help me in my final healing laps. I called my friend, a minister's wife, and told her about the posting, how badly I had wanted New York, how I had been so sure, and how I had been so wrong.

Here is the kind of friend you need when you are chipped and dented: no-nonsense but with a warm touch. Back when our husbands were studying to become priests, she ironed her secondhand dresses inside out so they lasted longer. She knew things. Darlene, too, had been so certain once, when her husband applied for a position that would have moved her close to her aging parents. I had cheered for them then, but they didn't get that job. Now Darlene listened to me. She read a poem to me. Mostly she said "I know." At the end she prayed for me.

I checked on the house around the corner; it was growing more and more remarkably orange as the improbable siding inched up the house. When Halloween came, giant black triangle eyes, a nose, and a smile were nailed on the pumpkin-orange house, filling up one whole side with a face. I smiled back.

*　　*　　*

In New York, my writer friends and I sat in The Modern, the restaurant at the Museum of Modern Art, where we had planned a special night out. We were midway through the writing class that had brought us to New York City. One of us, a *Saturday Night Live* alumna, knew the city from way back when and had suggested The Modern as a special place to eat.

It was staggeringly special: beautiful and spare and elegant, gray and white and silver. The sparkling water on the table sparkled more than any water that has sparkled anywhere ever. It practically burst out of its bottle. We all looked great in the perfect lighting. The tablecloth was heavy and pristine white. This whiteness wouldn't last long—I would spill something. But for now it was smooth and snowy under my fingertips, which were nervously tapping on the table.

The worry that was planted in me earlier that day as I scanned the menu online had now sprouted and grown. I'd hoped I had misunderstood the prices, but no: A four-course meal really did cost $158 a person, more than half of my wildly unrealistic $300 food budget for the week. There were several choices: hamachi marinated in sorrel vinaigrette, herb-roasted porcelet de lait, or maybe braised veal cheeks; but there was no bowl of soup or side order of fries you could order as you pretended you just weren't that hungry and made your plans to fill up with Shreddies later on.

We were a comedy teacher, a retired lawyer, a photographer, a restaurateur, and a minister's wife sitting around this gorgeous table. I didn't want to be the one to ruin the party and admit that I couldn't afford this meal; that the trip was already a stretch; that I had one kid in university, one on her way, and one who wanted skis. I certainly didn't belong there, although it was fun to visit.

The photographer, bless her freelance soul, questioned whether she was understanding the menu correctly. We all agreed that, yes, this was one very expensive place. Marsha, the former lawyer, conferred with the maître d', who was discretion itself wrapped in an exquisitely cut suit, the kind of elegance Brent would notice and appreciate. I wished I could take this man home to stand him in the corner, to be available when problems needed to be fixed by an extremely well-dressed person who spoke comfortingly in low tones and with such authority.

He ushered us into the less-expensive lounge and settled us into a row of chairs at the bar. There, arriving with my crispy chicken (a heavenly bargain at thirty-two dollars), were the biscuits—still as light as clouds, the butter spun from silk.

Each one of us ordered the exact same thing. As we sat at the beautiful, elegant bar, meals lined up like soldiers in front of us, we laughed at our mistake and our escape. I laughed harder than I had since I arrived. It was from the belly. There was a gift here. I could receive it and say thank you.

CHAPTER 11

Forgiveness

*Be kind and compassionate to one another, forgiving each
other, just as in Christ God forgave you.*

EPHESIANS 4:32

SO THERE I SAT, sipping a cup of hot tea with milk, listening to a podcast featuring writer Anne Lamott speaking about forgiveness. The house was empty, and by that I mean beautiful. Lamott says that "Earth is forgiveness school" and was about to whisper into my ear a story about learning to forgive her father. She was up to her neck in that big work of forgiving our parents for being as human as we are.

My phone rang. I hit pause on the podcast. It was my mother, calling to tell me stuff, including details about her salsa. She is joyful about all that is good. She told me she had chopped red and yellow peppers and there was chicken in her Crock-Pot for after church. She and my dad had racked up two funerals already that week and had more radishes than anyone could ever eat. They were ridiculously large, she said, and Dad had better not plant them again. It was unseasonably hot, and they were leaving for New Brunswick in the morning. Uncle Harry was home.

This was a news-receiving call. I knew I would have a quick moment or two at the end to blurt out some condensed updates of my own before my mother had to run. Sweet in a way, but also irritating to me on that day. I like to talk too. And because I can be so extra-irritable, I knew I might be irritated the entire day, and then my irritation would gather other annoyances together in a big bitter bunch, like those radishes. The things we feel and forgive are not always huge monsters. Sometimes they can fit under a bed or right into your pocket.

If Earth is forgiveness school, as Lamott says it is, then I spend most of my time in kindergarten.

Forgiveness is so difficult. It is a forest, thick and dark. And because the path is hard and long and not instant magic, it is the daily work of the Christian; a monotonous plodding toward an elusive but promised grace. Somehow we must find our way through to get to the light. Forgiveness is a command and also an invitation to a better life. It is a heavy path to a lighter soul.

I struggle to forgive. It is calculus to me, which back in school I knew not even to try. But we must try to forgive, because we know that unlike math, forgiveness actually is for our own good. We really will use it for our entire lives. It's not just for the good of the other person who did the small or maybe horrible thing but also for the good of our families and communities. It's actually for the good of the world, which sounds huge and like a song lyric. And those of us who are cynical—hurt and hard—are naturally suspicious of song-lyric things. But with forgiveness, it is all true.

Forgiveness is good. It is tough.

In my work as a Christian writer, I sometimes interview people about their experiences with forgiveness, just as other writers interview people about their new diets or their car crashes or something clever the person invented—like the lucky ducks who get to report on the iron that is also a coffee mug or the baby stroller/scooter hybrid. I have interviewed women and men who are the trapeze artists of faith, attempting astonishing feats of forgiveness while the rest of us watch from the ground with our popcorn, mouths hanging open.

There was Wilma, whose thirteen-year-old daughter was kidnapped on her way home from school, then killed. Years later, Wilma told me that forgiveness is as complicated as life and that it is daily work. You are never done forgiving. "It's never finished," she said. "You never finish cleaning the house."

There was Jerry, a man whose mother, wife, and daughter were killed by a drunk driver. I just could not imagine surviving that or forgiving my way through it. But this was back when I thought forgiveness was a onetime event and not the excruciating, stretched-out kind of thing that it usually is.

Like Wilma, Jerry told me that we are never really done

with the work of forgiving; that we can offer forgiveness, say it out loud, mean it, hand it over, and then feel so angry and betrayed a few seconds later. He said those hard moments of slipping backward into pain and hatred and sorrow are not failures of forgiveness but invitations to go deeper into those waters. We are allowed to feel what we are feeling, and then we get to forgive again.

Really, we are more vulnerable than we know to all that can go wrong in this world, and we are stronger than we can imagine to survive it. Forgiveness is also a survival technique.

Roy was a missionary whose sister was killed in a violent attack in South Africa. For years, Roy met regularly with his sister's killer to study the Bible in prison with him. Roy would fly from Canada to South Africa every few months for this reason. The convicted man became a Christian. He changed his plea from not guilty to guilty. The whole prison grew better and lighter, the warden said, because of the ripples of grace and light that shone from an old man visiting a murderer and forgiving him.

Then there's me: I'm still annoyed at the woman who alphabetized my bookcase without asking me, and at my niece, who cheats at Dutch Blitz by playing with both hands.

* * *

One Sunday morning when I was away from home at a writing course, I decided I wasn't going to attend church. I decided that not only was it okay to not go but that I deserved to eat pancakes somewhere and read a book instead.

As I walked across the campus of the university where I was staying, I saw a woman in a pretty dress and two young children climb out of a car. She had a purple throw over her shoulders and what looked like a bag of tricks to keep her kids amused. The little girl had a dress on. I noticed the boy's hair was sticking up in an unruly and sweet manner, despite what I guessed were his mother's best efforts. Sons are like that.

They are going to church.

I walked past them, free as a bird that doesn't attend church. Then I turned around again to watch, maybe to see whether I was right, and also because I felt a little bit lonely. For years I've taken a short nap on Friday afternoons, so now no matter where I am on a Friday, my eyes grow heavy at 1:00 p.m. And for years I have gone to church on Sunday mornings. On a Sunday morning my body expects to be in a pew with other people who have washed their hair and shown up, knowing there is more than just what we see around us.

So when the mom and two kids paused to chat with a couple who had just parked alongside them and climbed out of their car, I checked my phone. It was 10:29 a.m. I followed them. That's how I found myself at Real Life Community Church instead of Smitty's Pancake House.

Marilyn, the greeter just inside the door, offered me a warm hello and a firm handshake and pointed me down two flights of stairs. I walked past paper signs taped to doors and walls, telling me I was almost there. I entered the rehearsal hall of the arts building, where this campus church met every Sunday.

A man made a beeline for me, as people sometimes do at church when they spot someone new.

"Hi, I'm Bruce," he said.

"Hi, I'm Bruce," I said right back, because I had not yet had coffee or even a sip of water and maybe because I was already starting to think again about pancakes and my book. Bruce found this a little too funny, and I had to raise my voice to try to rein things in.

"Actually, my name is Karen," I explained. "I'm just visiting." Bruce pulled himself together and explained that a lot of people were away (as church people are always tempted to explain), and I answered his question about how I had heard about the church.

"I just followed that woman over there," I said, and I pointed to the mother. That's when I discovered that the woman who had caught my eye was a minister's wife like me, except with a magnetic power to pull people off the sidewalk, away from a delicious breakfast and into church.

"Have some coffee," he said and pointed me to the refreshments table.

I watched as Bruce sat beside Marilyn the greeter, who was now downstairs and clearly his wife. He slid his arm around her in that "I'm the captain and this is my first mate" kind of way that men have sometimes when they are sitting beside their wives in church, as if they were on a morning date. Sometimes I feel a little envious of this, because I have always sat alone in church—except when my three children were younger and had ants in their pants, as we used to say.

Bruce was the preacher that day. When he took his place behind the microphone and cleared his throat, beginning to speak, there was some noticeable chatter from the back of the room. Marilyn rose from her chair, strode to the source, and squashed that nonsense. I've done the same thing. I liked Marilyn even more, with her warm eyes and firm touch.

Bruce preached about forgiveness. He focused on Joseph, whose brothers had hated him, selling him into slavery because they were so jealous of him—and not just over the gorgeous coat he had, although that was part of it.

Years later, Joseph saved them when famine struck their land and they found themselves in his new homeland, hoping for a break. Joseph was their break. The brothers might have hated this for a bit until they saw it was their only way out. Here they were beholden to the person they had hurt probably more than anyone. Who wouldn't hate that?

Later Joseph told his brothers that what they had meant for bad, God had meant for good. He forgave them everything, something I assume he had been working on during those long nights during those stretched-out years of slavery and imprisonment. I imagine his forgiveness made his brothers feel both better and worse.

Bruce explained that Joseph saw the big picture. He was a big-picture forgiver. Joseph had cast his wound into the bigger story God was telling. "Stop looking at the wound," Bruce said. "Gaze at God."

Right. Thank you.

There in that church I had borrowed for the morning,

I felt a shift inside. I felt a little bit lighter thinking that my wounds could be cast into a bigger God-picture, when normally I would stare at them, poke at them, reopen them, and definitely report on them. I understood something new, which is actually something very old. Maybe I could be free as a bird after all.

* * *

One day, one of our sons picked up a crystal vase and smashed it down on the island in our kitchen. This son was angry at me for some mother crime. Probably I was angry at him first. That's usually how we rolled. The thick, ornate crystal shattered into a mound of glittering chunks. In an instant, the vase went from something to nothing. And our fight went from nothing to something.

My little bunch of daisies lay marooned on top of the island. The water spread like an ocean. I burst into tears and wailed, "That was a wedding present!" My son started to cry and then turned away and went upstairs to his room. I hate all those moments. It can feel like there are so many of them when you are in the middle of one of them.

I knew he hadn't meant to break the vase. Anger had swept him away on its raging river. That river is heavy with salt and is icy cold, and I often taste it too. I bunched up paper towels in my hand and pushed mounds of glass into the dustpan, then into the garbage with a heavy, damp thud. I knew I should have made him clean it up himself, suffer the consequences, blah blah blah—but I didn't want him to cut himself as he inevitably would, adding blood to our misery.

I have never really liked that vase.

I remember the dark blue box it arrived in—even the box required oohs and aahs—and the thick layers of tissue that swaddled it. I remember knowing I was supposed to love it because it was obviously expensive. It's the kind of thing you put your flowers in after you get married, when mason jars are no longer good enough.

The crystal vase was fancy and fussy, too heavy and important. The daisies had looked embarrassed standing in it. They knew they didn't fit. I rarely used the vase because it didn't match the flowers of my life. After I calmed down, I realized a little part of me was glad it was finally gone but that I would have preferred to have given it away in some grand gesture instead of losing it in a shattering fight.

I knew I had an opportunity to act out forgiveness, to show my son it really is a thing, that it is necessary and happens on purpose, as an act of our battered wills. I think we are required to teach the action and process of forgiveness to our children, just as we teach them to tie their shoelaces like bunny ears and to call their grandparents when they are teenagers.

The next morning, I went upstairs to his room with a glass of orange juice. He was warm and just waking, his hair stuck up like a forest, which made him look so young. His sheets were twisted around him like a hurricane had swept through his bed. I rubbed his back as he woke up in that messy bedroom that was so terrible. My son said he was sorry and that he felt horrible about the vase.

"How can you bring me juice after what I did?" he asked.
"I forgive you," I said. "I love you."

I didn't tell him that part of me was relieved I'd never have to force that vase to fit into our lives again. This was an opportunity to extend forgiveness, stretching it out between us like a rope and pulling him back toward me; to live something out and teach him something important; and to give him some love. "This is what we do," I said. "We forgive each other."

*   *   *

At church, the asking for and accepting of forgiveness is the lavish centerpiece on the table we all sit around. At our church we have a time of confession built in every Sunday, and we say the confession out loud together in the service every single week. It is projected in giant, unavoidable words on the wall, like a billboard. "We confess that we have sinned against you in thought, word, and deed, by what we have done, and by what we have left undone. We have not loved you with our whole heart; we have not loved our neighbors as ourselves."

So right there we are saying that when we explode at our mothers or think we want to shove Gloria down the stairs, it is God we have ultimately sinned against, not just Mom or Gloria. We can summon up all the cruddy things we did and said—and all the wonderful, loving things we didn't do or say—in the week that has just flown by. And we can tell God we are sorry.

This is not like emptying the garbage can on Sunday

just so we can fill it up again Monday through Saturday, although I can see why people might think this. The hope is that gradually, over time, some things we hear and experience from God in our lives will begin to rub off and rub in. Usually this kind of life and heart change works best when it flows from gratitude. And it happens in community, because we are in it together, standing around Jesus and learning. Because of what God has given us and shown us, we might eventually become a little bit more pleasant as human beings; a little more grateful and willing to share; and a little more like Jesus, holy and good.

But take note: If we start to notice how pleasant we are becoming, how generous and more flexible than, say, Marge over there, we send ourselves back to square one. But there is always a square one.

When it comes to matters of forgiveness, square one is often there under our feet because we have to deal with forgiveness so often. It is our work. It is ordinary and extraordinary. And forgiveness is especially difficult because it has to do with being wounded and with how hard some of those wounds are to recover from, especially the cuts that have happened in our most tender parts in our most tender times. So, wonderfully, we can also be forgiving of ourselves for how hard it is to forgive, but then still get on with the work of it.

Ultimately, I can give you a cup of forgiveness—and maybe you can offer one to me, too, because we swim in an ocean of it.

We are so vulnerable to each other and to all the meanness

there can be. That is when it is good to be in church—even when we don't really want to go that day—and be reminded that we ourselves are so deeply forgiven. We need to hear this every week. It is also good to hear the stories of those acrobats of the faith, such as Joseph, Wilma, Jerry, and Roy, contortionists of grace who forgave things we cannot even imagine enduring. They show us it is possible and it is good.

Personally, I always find it easier to forgive others when they come crawling toward me on their knees, crying and with a gift. But if they are the unacknowledging kind of person who might say things like "Why are you such a big baby?"—then of course the work of forgiveness is more difficult. I do know that each of us is asked to try to forgive whether the other person wants it or not, and even whether they know how badly they mucked up.

There was a time when once a year Brent and I would invite the whole church to the rectory for an open house on a Sunday afternoon during Advent. We knew that people liked to see how the old place was getting along (some would be making sure we weren't wrecking anything and would ask why we painted the kitchen cupboards blue). All of us would just enjoy each other's company. I love to cook. I would make little canapés and cheese balls and lay them out on pretty platters. I saw it as passing love around, in the form of cheese.

At one of these events, a woman sat in our living room for a couple of hours, then announced she was heading home. I encouraged her to wait a few minutes because I was about to wheel out the baked brie, always a hit.

"Haven't you had enough attention?" she asked, looking up at me from my favorite armchair.

My heart tells me I still have some work to do with this lady. I picture her perfectly in my mind, and not in a good way. I could call and tell her that I still think about what she said and how it hurt me and, if I remember correctly, how I stopped the brie baking for a few years, because I was crushed I had come across as so needy when I was trying to be really super great.

Maybe she would remember and say she was sorry. But she might say, "Didn't you move away?" or "So you still haven't had enough attention?"

This is the forgiveness risk. We might be in it all by ourselves. In those moments, we may have to remember that we have been given forgiveness as a holy chore and a command to obey. We receive forgiveness gladly, and we must give it freely; and it changes everything over and over again, like it was meant to. And as forgiveness works out first the grief and then the grace that is among us, we might also need to remember that it is for the good of our own big souls and our own tender hearts.

CHAPTER 12

Christmas

"The virgin will conceive and give birth to a son, and they will call him Immanuel" (which means "God with us").

MATTHEW 1:23

THE FIRST CHRISTMAS that I decorated the tree all by myself, without my children's help, at first I felt surprised and betrayed. I couldn't believe that no one wanted to help me, especially Holly. Who else can a mother count on if not her girl? I felt sad the kids had moved past seeing this as a magical launch to Christmas, a sacred part of their own celebration. But they were busy in their own rooms doing something fun that day.

Brent never really cared about decorating the tree and would do his best to avoid it. He carried out his annual duties of accompanying me to the tree lot; remarking on the height of the tree; tying it to the roof of our van; unloading it at home; forcing the boys to help him cut the trunk; wrestling it into the tree stand; going to buy a new tree stand because we had bought a cheap one the previous year and it had broken again; and watering the tree until he stopped caring and forgot.

Brent would appear again later in the season to toss the tree onto the side of the road for municipal pickup. This would happen the day after Epiphany, well into the first week of January. The tree itself had given up by then, shedding its needles by the fistful, forlorn in the corner of the room, a symbol of our stubbornness. We had stopped plugging the lights in, leery of fire and weary of Christmas. But waiting for Epiphany—the celebration of the wise men visiting Jesus and his parents—was our way, at Brent's urging, of proclaiming that Christmas lasts longer than a day. "It's an entire season!" he would say. The wise men mattered, but by then I couldn't wait for it all to end.

So the day the kids declined to help me decorate, it dawned on me I could have a pretty tree that year. I could consider color and spacing. I wouldn't have to sneak around after they had gone to bed and rearrange things, moving the giant Styrofoam snowmen heads from front and center to side and low. I thought of the pictures in magazines of trees with clustered decorations, elegant little trios of color-coordinated glass balls nestled together at the end of green branches. I could do that.

"It's okay!" I shouted up the stairs in case anyone was about to change their mind and charge down. "It's all good!"

I took my time. I listened to Christmas carols and sang

along. I unwrapped ornaments from their little tissue paper homes and laid them all out on the couch before I placed each one thoughtfully on the tree—mostly on the front as it turned out.

I awarded positions of prominence to the family heirloom pieces, those tiny glass balls from our respective childhoods, ideal for hanging together on the ends of branches in delicate little groups of three, as instructed and inspired by the people who know what they are doing.

After an hour or so, I stood back to admire. I sighed with contentment at how lovely and sophisticated our tree looked. Gorgeous.

A few peaceful seconds passed. Then my beautiful tree fainted forward and fell flat at my feet, spilling water and shattering glass balls. The kids heard the crash and came running. I burst into tears.

Brent appeared and asked, "What happened? Why are you crying?"

It was everything I hated about Christmas—the striving and the failing; the tyranny of the non-Jesusy parts; the seasonal aloneness that comes during this busy church season; and the way I consistently set the cooking, gifting, decorating, and activity bar much higher than time or talent would ever suggest is wise, as if I had to prove something.

*   *   *

I know from the boxing movies I have been forced to watch that for every boxer there is a coach—the cheerleader who leans into the face of the weary fighter and shouts encouragement while forcing water down his protégé's throat with a weird bottle and straw. "You can do it! Drink!" Then the coach thrusts the boxer back out into the ring for another round, and soon the boxer appears in the chair again for more nourishment and encouragement.

I am the coach. Brent is the boxer. The Christmas season is round after round of special services and events, amazing sermons one after another, and often a few pastoral emergencies thrown in to tip everything further off-kilter. Then the boxer finally comes home very late on Christmas Eve—after the coach and the family guests, who have come to us because we can never leave to go visit them, really want to go to bed.

He arrives after all the gifts are wrapped, the breakfast casserole everyone loves is made, the stockings are stuffed, and everyone else in the whole world is asleep. He might glance around and remark about how messy things are. He sighs, slumps, and asks the coach for some of those puffy cheese appetizers he loves so much. The boxer wants the coach to sit beside him, hold his hand, and talk to him for a few minutes, which would be alluring just about any other time. The coach tries to be tender even then, because it's Christmas for the pastor, too, after all, and look how busy he's been. Plus maybe his mother and father are there watching.

This is what Christmas is like in a clergy household: like everyone else's Christmas, only worse.

* * *

My pre-Christmas anxiety usually began in early November and increased with each candle that was lit at our table on each of the four Sundays in Advent. Lighting the Advent candles, meant to slow down the season and fill us with holy anticipation, reminded me less of grace and more of grind. Brent would see my stress building like a wave about to crash into our family, and he would try to alert me to it, which did not help. I worried anyway. Plus we'd have an argument about my worry-denial, which made it even worse.

I worried about the expectations of the family members who visited. I marveled at the clergy friends we had who would tell family they could not come during Christmas—ever—because it was just too crazy a season. Brent and I couldn't turn our parents away, and we didn't want to; but to see others erecting such clear boundaries in recognition of how demanding this season could be in the home of a minister was awe-inspiring.

I worried about money. The long list of people we needed to buy for crushed me.

And I worried that our gifts were never good enough.

Christmas weighed me down under all the special thises and thats, the need for it to sparkle so it would be magical for my family. How we celebrated Christmas did not feel like it matched with what we celebrated, and the spiritual disconnect stumped me every year.

Plus my husband was gone, and everything seemed to

depend on me. All the women I knew carried the brunt of the season like a giant stuffed sack, just waiting for Boxing Day so they could be the one to collapse on the couch.

Christmas done the crazy way is a woman problem and a spiritual challenge, as well as a logistical issue if you are generally horrible at arts and crafts, decorating, and wrapping gifts so they look great. "Here," my mother-in-law once said during a pre-Christmas visit to their home, "take this Scotch tape home with you so you have some when I come and visit."

* * *

Sometimes I resented that my husband was off making Christmas special for others by officiating the services that were sentimental and nostalgic for them and, yes, lovely with all the candles and music—while I was next door in the rectory trying to make it special for our little family.

It embarrasses me to admit that. The confession adds to my seasonal shame. I wish I were a better minister's wife who never thinks such things and who, time after time, fully embraces the opportunity to serve at home while he serves at church. And I wish I always had Scotch tape.

If I were better, this would all be easier.

There is a recurring dream I have where I am in a large church I do not recognize, and I can't find Brent. I wander around the sprawling building, one room leading into another, looking for my husband until I stumble into a service that has already begun. Sometimes when I finally find him in my dream, he doesn't recognize me. This is a dream staggering in its unfairness to my caring husband and to any loving church of which we have ever been a part, and yet it comes back every once in a while and ruins my day.

Brent has his own version of a nightmare where he finds himself high up in the pulpit of a strange church, without a sermon note to be had, a huge congregation expectant and eager before him. We can't help what we dream. The first time he told me about this, waking and warm beside me, I felt so tender toward him.

* * *

One Christmas Eve I stood at our open freezer in the cellar of the rectory, shaping vanilla ice cream into balls so I could make little snowmen. My hands dripped with melting ice cream and ached with cold, and I wondered why I was doing this. I still had seven more snowmen to shape for the guests upstairs, who had not requested ice cream snowmen for dessert. They had never even heard of them. I had seen a picture in a magazine and thought, *That looks easy and fun!*—a warning signal that what was to follow wouldn't be easy and probably not fun.

Eventually I allowed myself to question the type of Christmas that made me take to my bed at two in the afternoon, hiding from relatives and texting my daughter to please bring me a cup of hot tea. *How would Jesus plan his own birthday if he were in charge of a twelve-day-long festival that never seemed to end?* I wondered.

We took action. We shrank the number of gifts we bought

for our children to three, modeling our giving after those wise men; and we bought better gifts we thought would last longer and hold more meaning. But the truth is, kids of a certain age would prefer to get lots of junky gifts instead of three good ones. Trust me—I know.

Still, we pushed through. Some years we had each of our children choose something out of a charity catalog to give in honor of Jesus. Our kids were drawn like flies to dairy cows and entire barnyards full of animals, which we could not afford. The message we were sending became confusing: "You can be generous, but not really." We kept tweaking.

We knew we were better stewards of creation and of our resources when we didn't buy junk. For Brent's parents, we shifted toward giving the gift of time and an outing. We also came up with simpler ideas for my own mom and dad.

No one complained. Christmas began to make a little more sense.

* * *

Things can be very sad in our lives. We can have several dreary months in a row, and who among us loves November? To claim one or two weeks every year to remember there is hope, that love was born into flesh for us, and that it's okay to pause and spend entire days visiting and feasting and watching movies and playing games—this is good, and it matters.

Lighting tall taper candlesticks on a table set for our family plus company is something I love, and resisting the temptation to believe everyone else is doing even that in a more elegant way is also something I must do. *I must stop comparing*, I remind myself every year.

The desire to savor and not just survive the birth of our Savior is an important and tender impulse of the heart. What does it mean to celebrate the birth of Jesus in a way that does not make us want to apologize to him? This is my abiding Christmas question.

As our church congregation discussed how we could be more intentionally missional in our community, we decided to cancel the annual Advent open house our family hosted for the church and instead open our home to the people on our street. We delivered invitations door-to-door and waited nervously on the day of the event to see whether anyone would show up.

Thirteen people did show up that year. Conversation drifted from community news to the history of our busy street to updates on the general business, health, and well-being (or not) of the neighbors who hadn't come, and probably hadn't realized they would be talked about quite so much. We introduced carol singing, and to our surprise, everyone gamely joined in. Most of the people in our living room did not go to church, and the hour or so of singing was a kind of joy to the world, right there in our house with Bill and Gwen from next door sitting on the extra chairs we pulled into the room, and Shannon from across the road perched on our worn couch.

* * *

The Christmas turkey has never been my friend. It is a problem to be solved, math and mess. I circle around it, raw on my counter, and weigh my options. In trying to solve the problem of the turkey, I have cooked it upside down in the quest for a juicy breast, soaked it in a bucket of brine, filled it with homemade or boxed stuffing, left it unstuffed, and roasted it on the day before and the day after Christmas.

I have begun a pot of turkey soup, stock bubbling away to less and less all day long until the pot was abandoned and left on a cold stove all night. I would toss it out in defeat. To do all that other work and then make soup? It was just too much. I replaced turkey with prime rib, only to discover that the actual fact of the turkey, big and bold, seems essential to Christmas.

Then one year Holly said, "Our church should hold a Christmas dinner for the community." Brent struck a committee. We all met in the church basement and divvied up jobs, and Christmas Day changed forever and for so much better.

With a worship service on Christmas morning, our family shifted to opening presents after Christmas dinner, late in the afternoon. The boys grumbled, "Great idea, Holly!" and then shone like lights flicked on in a darkened room. They visited well with the mostly lonely seniors from the community who had come, happy to find company and a good meal.

Elderly veterans told their war stories, and some shared sad accounts of family gone wrong. Old scars mean new wounds at Christmas. Our church basement became a first-aid clinic, and listening was the medicine—that and a few hours of eating and singing carols together, led by Brent and a little group playing guitar and a portable keyboard set up in the corner near the Sunday school supply cupboard.

In a way, it was ironic that adding something this huge into our Christmas celebrations lightened it all up. It was a chore that counted, a busy full of beauty. Working together with our church family to serve was one way to have Christmas make more sense. Our work to feed and be present with others brought value because it was not about us—and that is always when we are especially blessed. Giving really is receiving as it turns out. We just need to remember this again and again when we lose our minds a little bit at times like Christmas.

But it was more than just serving at the dinner that made it special—it was the partaking. It was the feasting that fed us. The first year, I still came home and cooked our own turkey. As I pulled it out of the oven, I was struck by the superfluousness of this big awkward bird. Why wasn't the only table we needed that long table where we had just sat with strangers in our church basement?

This became an important theological question for our family. Were we eating with our neighbors or not? Was the food that was good enough for them good enough for us, or wasn't it? Were we all equally lost and found, or weren't we? That was the last Christmas I roasted a turkey of our own (hallelujah and amen to that). We became both hosts and guests at all the church dinners that followed.

A few years in, we moved from that small town to a larger city and a larger church that had served Christmas dinner for decades. This dinner was different from the one we had come from; it welcomed more people without homes or who were harshly marginalized with very little income. Loneliness was not their only problem. They arrived in the warm church hall out of the freezing cold of Christmas Day—for singing, shelter, turkey, and I think tenderness.

My visiting parents were put to beautiful use as they sat at the end of a long table and, in the fullness of their grandparentness, held the happy baby of a young family who had just moved into the city and knew no one. So much better than sitting in my living room drinking eggnog and waiting for me to snap.

This was Christmas, truly. This was Jesus, who had arrived on this day in the manger, and, yes, in our city, here in this room, and was making everything in the world make sense, finally. We left Christmas dinner full, not needing anything else from that strange and somehow sacred day.

We are all guests. Jesus is our host at a vast and endless table we ourselves do not build with all our striving, but he does with his grace and with his goodness. We are the invited and the welcomed to this quirky party. We can relax. And yes, we can even enjoy it.

CHAPTER 13

Moving

The LORD himself goes before you and will be with you;
he will never leave you nor forsake you. Do not be afraid;
do not be discouraged.

DEUTERONOMY 31:8

I DID NOT MOVE AWAY FOR GOOD from the home I grew up in, or the street I grew up on, the entire time it took me to grow. I went there as a newborn straight from the hospital to live at the mercy of my older sister, lying in wait for me in her lair. I left for the last time in my wedding dress to meet Brent, waiting for me at the front of a chapel.

My parents long ago sold that house and moved to the country. I still like to drive by it. The tree that was small is big. The house that was big is small. How did we fit? There is the house where old Mrs. Johnson lived; she is long gone. Our cat had an emotional affair with her and spent hours sitting on her doorstep, gazing hopefully at her screen door.

How I longed to move, back then—to pack everything I owned into cardboard boxes and watch my life be swept away into a big empty truck, knowing it could be unpacked and made new somewhere else, maybe somewhere better.

When Brent and I bought our first house, we moved from the rectory just around the corner and down two blocks to a brick house on the busiest street of our small town. *That is such an ugly house,* I used to think as I drove by it on the way straight out of town or to swimming lessons or soccer practice. Forest green awnings hung heavy over front-bedroom windows, breaking up a stretch of orange brick. We swore we'd modernize it once we moved in, but we never did.

"Do you think this is your forever home?" a friend once asked me in a dreamy voice. She had little children, so she still talked like that. Plus she was not married to a minister, so she could count on living in the same community for years and years.

"I doubt it," I answered, even though I had fallen in love with the family room and that wall we painted butternut rum just because we wanted to. And I still miss the Ping-Pong table and how good I was at playing. It was a secret bonus skill I whipped out just when our kids thought they had me all figured out.

Ministers and their families don't really have forever homes. We stayed fifteen years in the Ping-Pong-table town, the longest by far and so far. We brought our children up mostly in that one town.

When they were small, we lived in the same charming

old rectory where every minister from that congregation and his family lived. A long line of ministers' wives had cooked big meals in its small kitchen and welcomed church people into the beautiful living room with the fireplace that did not work. Go out the door and cross the lawn, and there you were at the church.

When the kind retired man who took care of the church's gardens noticed how untended the rectory's gardens looked in comparison, he offered to weed ours too. "Yes, sure," I said. But gardening was something I looked forward to doing all by myself one day at our own house, finally. I imagined wearing a floppy hat and cotton gloves and rising up to greet a visitor who caught me unaware as I worked the dark soil in my khakis, like in the movies. All that peace and pleasure.

Then I discovered that gardening is hard, hot work that you do all scrunched up, on your knees. All those people I had observed over the years, digging around in their front yard, might have been hating every second of it, like I did. We think so much is better somewhere else, and that gardens grow just by wishing they would.

But I liked that at our own house, members of the women's group did not suddenly appear at my backdoor window to ask questions. My children's play area did not have a door that led in and out of the church hall for the shaking out of table-cloths or emptying of coffeepots. We could paint whatever we wanted whenever we wanted—and not ask permission to do a single solitary thing. People didn't show up looking for Brent as often, and if they did, they usually really needed him.

Moving from the rectory to our own house gave us some space; but as it turns out, it did not move us to another planet. You stay mostly the same when you move, despite what you hope.

*　*　*

"How does it work?" people ask, about the moving. I think they really want to know if we had a choice. Did we want to leave this church? This town? Them?

Often, yes, because it is time. It is time to leave for the sake of the church where the minister might grow stale, like bread left out on the counter, dry and then stiff and easily snapped in two. Sometimes it is just time for everyone, and that time makes itself known as clear as the water that moves you forward on a strong and resolute river. *It is time to go,* the river says, *and over there is where you are going ashore.* It can be that obvious.

Sometimes it feels like God says, in an ordinary way, "Okay, you can go now," like you do when things are just over—as complete as you can make them, and you know it. The dance has ended. In that place between places, which on one day feels like a desert and on another might feel like a garden, the minister and his wife discuss the coming and the going quietly, lying in bed beside each other, and pray and speculate and wonder and read job postings and apply, just like anyone else does when they find a job they think they want. And then, in a few months or two years or ten, you move.

*　*　*

I am just following you around.

Maybe it was after we left Saskatchewan—that place I thought I wouldn't like, which won me over and loved me so well—when I finally said this out loud to Brent. Probably I was surrounded by broken boxes and maybe looking for a light bulb. I would have been tired, which is when we most often say these kinds of things.

It is true that all our moves were about his calling—his calling and my following. How terrible it must have been for him to discover I sometimes had this feeling of following and never leading, of lagging behind and not standing beside. Saying it out loud helped. I aired out my feeling like a bedsheet hung on a line.

"I trust you." I would say that to God as I stood in a room either just emptied or about to be filled. When we left one place and arrived at another, saying it reminded me that I did and I could and I would. And if I trusted God, it helped me trust Brent and our decision making, and that there would be something in that move for me as well.

I have a two-drawer file cabinet I move with me, filled with interview notes, kids' report cards, and story ideas I probably won't ever pursue as a writer; but I carry them still. I weed the files down so they can grow again. Depending on the house, I might have a corner of a family room or a spare bedroom to call my office.

I wanted a career that would fit into a backpack, and it is writing. *I can move again.* I can move for Brent's work; I can help him when he needs me, which I'd always wanted to do anyway because of love, and because I can. *This is an adventure.*

But of course things were never that simple. There was always me bursting into tears on the Sunday Brent announced our leaving in church, right at the end of the service. This, just when everybody had been thinking they could get downstairs to the tea and blueberry muffins or shoot straight over to Swiss Chalet.

And there were the friends I made. Maybe they would cry, too, and our sadness combined became even more difficult.

There was also the worry of wonder: *Are we leaving too soon? Too late?* That would be me mostly, not Brent. He always felt certain, even when he felt badly.

There were apologetic emails and hasty calls to the friends I couldn't tell until we worked our way through the process. Ministers can't really tell people they are thinking of leaving, because then people feel like they are already gone.

There was the comforting of our children or the taming of their excitement. "Good. Now I'll have more time to read," said Erik, moving from city to town.

We said goodbye to the parents who had lost their child, the wife who had lost her husband.

There were the women in the Bible study group and the moms in the playgroup, the friendly librarian and the stern one.

There was the very old couple who had thought Brent would be the one to do their funerals, to bury them. Then they realized it would likely be a minister they hardly knew saying those words and leading that singing.

There was the Catholic priest who had become our friend.

For the community newspapers I wrote for, another reporter moved along.

There was the last Santa Claus parade we marched in, likely forever, because it takes a long time to become a part of that type of thing.

There was the slow and awful emptying of a house we had tried hard to make our home; it turned out to be just walls and a roof after all.

Where in the world did all this crap come from? I always wondered. And what is it that always remained? Odd socks, that's what. Single socks were everywhere as the rest of the house marched itself into boxes, the mystery of where they had been hiding solved under beds and rugs and books and in dusty, dim corners.

The last time we moved, I walked out of our house for the final time with a teapot in one hand and my winter boots in the other. I shoved my toothbrush deep into one of the boots for safekeeping.

It is so much hard work to move. And it is so much heart work.

* * *

I visited South Sudan in 2012, back when it was the newest country in the world, just barely a year old. But hope had already started melting away from that brightly lit candle. I was a writer visiting refugee camps. I could see the tops of the tents from the air as our plane landed, and how organized it all was, with lanes and neighborhoods. I saw community in the despair and the uprootedness of the people who were there, and this surprised me.

The refugees had made homes, because that's what people do wherever they go: They build nests, especially for their children, even when they have fallen hard from unfriendly skies. Wearing flip-flops and using their washbasins and whatever little else they have, mothers piece together homes from scratch anywhere they have to. Dirt floors are swept daily. Markets bud into life. Grandmothers gather scattered grandchildren under their wings, as they do so fiercely and so well, everywhere and all the time. Congregations form and meet under sprawling, sheltering trees or in small, hot rooms with tin roofs and leaning walls. Pastors teach and comfort scattered flocks.

There in the camps, people gather their power and their prayers and create community and home once again. Teachers push kids to read and teach them how to think in this unexpected makeshift and unasked-for new life. Their callings are lived out in the most difficult of places.

How can such pain and such beauty exist in one place, in one spread-out homemade home?

In northern Uganda a few years later, they didn't call them camps; they were settlements, because settling was what these refugees, who had fled from an even further disintegrated South Sudan, were encouraged to do. *Here are some seeds—plant a garden. Here is the well—-draw some water. Here is a school—send your children. There is the doctor—go and get better.*

As visiting journalists, our job was to gather stories like berries and then go home and bake a pie. We were to give people a taste of things so they could understand and maybe they would do something. At least they would know.

Jane, a grandmother, stood tall and stately in the middle of her plot of land, her square footage of dignity.

Here, there is dignity everywhere.

A throw rug, like some of us have in our living rooms, was spread out flat on the ground near her hut. Her grandchildren perched there like little birds, giggling shyly at the strangers in their space. Always know, foreign visitor, that you are being laughed at with your bulging pockets and your big hat, because of how sweaty you are and how you droop and sway, how you scribble in your little notebook and cling feverishly to your water bottle.

Three of us asked Jane questions about her five-day walk to safety. Then we asked, "Jane, what is life like here?" We hoped she would say "better" so we could feel so much better, for her and for ourselves.

The guy with the camera, doing his job, asked whether he could go into her little hut to take pictures. I wanted to see, too, but I would not go into her home and look around, not even for a good story. I wouldn't ask a neighbor I happened to meet on my street if I could go in and look around her house, so I didn't do it there either.

Instead I imagined the blankets, the shelf, the basin, the book. I pictured Jane arranging those very few things she had carried with her and those things she would have received when she arrived, like a water container and a bar of soap. She would have arranged them in a way that would make her grandchildren feel the best, her whole world shrunk into this space. Maybe there was a photograph or two stuck into the mud walls with a tack.

I stayed outside with Jane, and for a minute it was just the two of us.

"Do you have any friends here?" I asked.

"Yes," she answered, "in my church." We smiled at each other.

You are so strong.

Home really is where the heart is, just like they say. Your heart can be in more than one place at a time, especially if it is broken.

* * *

I drove Thomas to school in the new city we lived in, dragging and dropping him to spend the day among strangers who, so far, were all horrible weirdos. In the beginning I picked him up every single day. I thanked God again that I worked from home so I could do this for him.

This move had been the most painful ever—maybe because we had stayed in that one town for so long—first in the rectory, then in our own house. Thomas, our sixteen-year-old son, had the big rug of home ripped out from under his feet. Erik had moved already, off to university at seventeen. Holly left two days before we did, off to a Bible college in Costa Rica, backpack full and heavy.

Before she left, she and I had done our liturgy of leaving—the way we said goodbye to the places we left. We walked through our house and remembered what we did in each room, saying thank you out loud. This time we walked through our whole town, which felt like our whole home.

Thank you, post office, where we received our letters and sometimes a big package from my mother, marked up with "Hi!" and "Love you!"

Thank you, grocery store, for the milk and the bread. And thank you, library, for everything.

We thanked our way around our town until we almost stepped on a dead squirrel in the middle of the sidewalk. We grabbed each other and screamed, and laughed until we cried. Then we walked back to our home, already torn apart.

For Thomas especially and mostly, this was a dragon of a move. I encouraged him to stay at school for lunch. "Dig deep!" I chirped. It was my new slogan. "If you're there in the library or the cafeteria or wandering the halls, you will be able to make friends," I reasoned. He told me if he followed my advice he would be the biggest weirdo at school and would never make any friends.

This could have been the case. Maybe I really did not know what I was talking about. I knew mostly about moves with younger children across shorter distances. We had uprooted him halfway through his junior year of high school.

We thought this would be better than starting a new school as a senior, like it would be better to have your arm chopped off quickly instead of chewed off slowly.

We believed God had called Brent to this church. And with that assurance, we believed that Thomas would be okay. We prayed he would be. We had asked for a green light from all our nearly grown children for Brent to even apply. The problem with green lights, though, is you don't always know what's on the other side of the intersection.

This was the move that would mark Thomas, for better or for worse. The move in which much was required. It was the sacrifice of the daily presence of lifelong friends, the halls at school already mapped out in his mind, the science classroom where he sat in his boxer shorts for an hour to earn twenty dollars from his friends, and the teacher who didn't notice.

We are here for you, we promised him, even as we knew we were the last people he wanted to hang out with in the dead of winter in a brand-new city. We told him what we had seen and heard before and knew to be true: When God calls Brent to something new, the rest of us do not stand outside the call and hear nothing. The calling covers us all somehow. God always meets us in a new place.

This is a true and tender thing, even if it's impossible to believe when you are sixteen. God is there behind us in our past, and he is with us in our present and stands before us in our future. But to know this you must live it, maybe a couple of times over. We all will learn eventually that love does not move away, even if we do. It moves along with us.

So we set up our son's bedroom, first and best. We bought a large TV for the family room that Thomas helped pick out—a football field of a TV. This was bribery. It was fun, but it did not cure his aloneness.

What if this never does get better for him? My fear galloped past my faith.

Each day felt like it had twelve extra hours. I jumped out of my skin with the *ping ping ping* of incoming texts. "Dig deep. Stay put," I wrote back. "You never know what good thing is about to happen. Just do the work and get out. You're almost done for the day. It will be okay. I love you. We love you. Let's go to a movie tonight."

My most prayerful friends prayed. Maureen checked in with me regularly on Facebook Messenger. "When I pray for Thomas, I see his face in front of me," she wrote. This comforted me like a pillow and a blanket.

"Today was a good day," Thomas said sometimes when he came home from school, like a mercy. Some people would not admit to their life-wreckers that they had a good day. His heart was tender enough to want to comfort us with progress. *Thank you.*

I met up with Christine at a conference. Our paths had crossed before, but we had never sat at the same round table for lunch, eating vegetarian wraps. One of the good things for me in this move was that I got to go to conferences and lectures and events happening in universities and all around the city. I let my joy over this spill out in small splashes only, for my son's sake. Christine is older than me, lovely and serene and recovering from cancer.

She asked about our move. I opened my heart to this woman I barely knew, her soft hair growing back in, so clearly a survivor of harder things than our family has ever gone through. "It has been very difficult for our son," I said.

She reached for my hand. She did not say what so many said: "What?! You moved your son in the middle of his junior year?"

Thank you.

"What's his name?" she asked. I told her.

"I will pray for him," she promised. I believed her.

"Resilience," she said. "That is what you are giving your son." I thanked her.

"His whole life, this gift will serve him," my wise friend said. *Please.*

* * *

Spring brought rugby. A good high school with a winning rugby team is why we bought a house that was too big in a neighborhood that was too quiet. It was the least we could do.

Inch by inch, our son made friends. *Who could resist this funny boy?*

I updated Maureen. "But don't take your foot off the gas," I told her.

One evening, Olivier showed up in our kitchen, as pleasant a surprise as a bowl of cherries. Then Alex. Later, Julien. Brent and I tried to be friendly but not strange. Engaging but not too chatty. Whenever anyone was there we vacated the TV with joy (Brent not so much) and watched our show on my iPad, huddled together on our bed so Thomas could entertain downstairs. I paid for pizza.

Months in, Maureen and her husband, Bruce, arrived for an overnight visit. They had known this son since he was new, wrapped in a soft blanket in my arms. Maureen opened her arms wide and Thomas stepped into them, receiving. She hugged him hard, like another mother. "I have been praying for you, and I won't stop." He laughed that warm chuckle of his and hugged her back.

It will be okay.

All this pain and healing and all these moves have turned us into wanderers. There is so much wandering throughout the Bible: movement, shifting, and following. Trusting, leaving, and arriving. We follow God and love follows us. We have lived in so many houses, and I have created so many homes. I always set up the kids' bedrooms first, and ours at the very end, when everything else is done.

I unpack my books and say, "Oh, hello again," then leave some in piles so I can reach them quickly when I need them and just admire their straight, smooth spines from across the room when I don't. They come with me everywhere. So do the photos on the fridge, but only on the sides. Brent is a man who likes his fridge door clean, and I give him that. The sides are a jumble of photos and magnets and scraps of memories. He gives me that.

In this new house, there is sometimes a rugby ball on the kitchen floor, and Thomas throws it up in the air repeatedly, even though we tell him not to repeatedly. He catches it again in hands that are almost a man's. Holly's coat rests in a heap on the floor. She has arrived back to *this* home from her Bible college, and we are so thankful.

Brent hangs the painting of a woman watering her plants with her black cat watching, bought for me for ten dollars so many years ago at a yard sale in Saskatoon. We had it reframed here at a little shop we found in a mall right after we moved. I appreciate it again, bordered by its new frame, like a new home.

"Is it straight?" he asks me.

"I think so," I say, squinting.

"Is it centered?" he asks.

"Looks like it," I say, hoping.

"Well, it is or it isn't," he says.

And this is the drama we act out on every wall in every house on every road in every town we live in. We set things up, placing pieces in this house, which is our home for now.

Brent pats the dining room table as he walks by it. We've been lucky with the dining rooms ever since we bought this big long table with two leaves; it can seat so many when everyone squishes together on all four sides.

Brent calls home almost daily to ask who will be at dinner.

He wants as many of our kids as possible to be there—as often as possible—before they are all gone, setting and sitting at their own tables.

We eat together as often as we can, even though sometimes we argue and someone storms off; even when I've made it simple, and we are eating just cut-up carrots and peppers and bread torn into chunks. Even if the cheese is just cheddar and nothing fancier than that.

On this night, we've run out of milk. I'd forgotten to buy more, so I will do that first thing tomorrow.

This is our home for today, for at least a part of our journey—the journey God has given us as a gift, with open, soft hands that intend no harm. We will let our roots sink down and find our way.

CHAPTER 14

Holiness

It is written: "Be holy, because I am holy."

1 PETER 1:16

WHEN BRENT WAS IN HIS FIRST PARISH, and I was in my first pregnancy, we attended a birth preparation class held at a local community center. We thought we were young—until we went to the first class. After that we felt old, like we were grandparents having a baby.

Some of the couples were just out of high school. Brent and I were definitely the only ones just out of seminary. We kept our mats and ourselves to the corner of the room. Kevin and Nicole, another couple there learning how to breathe through labor, invited us over for dinner, and once or twice for euchre; but eventually they gave up on us with that.

Nicole and I drank tea together often during those long days of new motherhood in a tiny town. Our firstborns were first best friends, toppling over on baby blankets that the women of that town had pieced together and quilted as gifts.

"If I could be religious like you are, I would be—because you can't tell," Nicole said to me one afternoon.

"Oh. Thank you," I said, and I meant it to my bones.

But maybe I would not have won the Minister's Wife of the Year award.

Although I had disappointed Nicole by never remembering the suit in euchre, she thought I was okay. We weren't that different.

But am I letting the team down? I wondered. I did not mention Jesus as we talked about diaper brands and life plans and our husbands and our sisters and recipes. But I was my true self with Nicole. We really liked each other, like good friends do.

I had been made holy because he is holy, even though I clearly was not presenting as holy—or was I? What did that even mean? I trusted that I was a "restored image bearer," as Brent says, and I hoped this made me an even better friend to Nicole than I would have been otherwise—and to anyone else who might invite me over on a Wednesday morning and let me sit on their leather couch.

* * *

When Brent was in seminary, he took an evangelism class from a professor who told him, after reading his assignments, that in terms of faith at least, he would not want what Brent had.

The problem began when the professor said that Christians should smile, even when they go to the dentist, and maybe especially then.

"But what if you're terrified of the dentist?" Brent asked. "Why be fake?"

That is when his evangelism professor said to him, "Brent, I would not want what you have."

I would not be hired as an evangelism professor anywhere in the world. But I think this professor was wrong. People will know we are Christians by our love and not by our pretending.

Instead of pretending to love the dentist, it is better to ask the dental receptionist what her name is, and then remember she is Dorothy. And don't bite her head off, even when you are so afraid and nervous and when the billing isn't correct. Be set apart by being fully present. Don't be mean. Be different because you know such a big love, and love God back by loving Dorothy, who is sitting there waiting for you every time you have an appointment. Admit that you're nervous. Ask her for some reassurance. Remember, Dorothy can spot a phony a mile away. Say thank you often, because you have good manners, and maybe eventually you can invite Dorothy to church or tell her about Jesus in a way that doesn't freak her out.

* * *

We grow, like plants. We are not the messes we once were; at least we shouldn't be if we are living in the Light. Being made holy changes us both in the twinkling of an eye and eventually and slowly. It is instant and gradual. If we receive

God's love for us and bask in it, we will change. We will grow. But it can be slow.

When someone shows up at my door with a little plant, I know it is doomed. I feel sorry for it, and secretly annoyed with the person who brought over this clay pot of guilt. I will forget about this plant, and then remember it and underwater or overwater it, often both. Sometimes I just toss the plants right out into the backyard to put us all out of our misery.

Jesus, though, is the nurturing Gardener of our hearts. He tends us, and so we attend to him. He grows us. He is seed, soil, and sun.

Henri Nouwen wrote about three movements of the spiritual life in his book *Reaching Out*. He says that after a reordering of our relationship with God, "reaching out to our fellow human beings" is the second kind of transformation we undergo in our spiritual lives. Nouwen described it as a movement "from hostility to hospitality."

Our natural selfishness and desire to take care of mostly just ourselves abates, just a bit. Hospitality is "one of the richest biblical terms that can deepen and broaden our insight in our relationships to our fellow human beings," he wrote.

I love this confirmation of movements in our spiritual lives. Take heart; there is movement. And if we are moving in the right direction, it is a profound shifting away from the self and toward others. Our hearts are being changed, even on the slow days.

*   *   *

"They leave everything to come to nothing." That's what Fatima, the translator, said at the airport as we waited impatiently for a Syrian refugee family to land and begin their new lives in Canada.

The churches in our town had fundraised for months to bring, in the end, four families to our community. They hosted Syrian meals, held an art show built on the theme of refuge, auctioned off birdhouses decorated by artists, and stood at the entrances of grocery stores to gather donations.

Finally the first family arrived, and Holly and I almost danced as we waited. Then Fatima said what she said, and I realized that this was one of the most exciting and rewarding days of my life, and maybe one of the worst days for the eighteen-year-old mother of three about to walk through the arrival doors at the airport.

In fact, the mom was pale and silent when we finally saw her, her tiny hand clinging to the cart that held their few small bags. She looked like a child. I reminded myself she was a mother like me and also not at all like me, because she had lost her home and her family and her whole life and had just arrived in a terrifying new place, greeted by a bunch of delighted strangers hopping with glee. In that moment it seemed silly that I had downloaded the iTranslate app earlier in the day. *What was I thinking?*

I almost cried because I was so happy they had arrived, that we had accomplished this mighty thing. But the thought of how ridiculous and over the top my tears would seem to this young mom stopped me. It was for her to weep, not me. I pulled myself together like an unmade bed.

What I had seen in our church leading up to this night—the committee meetings, the planning, the praying, and the waiting—reminded me again that faith comes alive in the doing. Holy is and holy does. When we serve, we live. Our faith makes more sense then, and so do our churches. Bringing refugee families to town is one of the holiest things our church had ever done.

We all know that it is so good and rich to serve, but we sometimes forget this because we are so busy, or because it gets so cold in the winter or too hot in the summer, or because the timing is never perfectly perfect for us. But faith with works is an alive thing: delicious, full, and plump, like a ripe orange bursting with fresh smell and sweet juice. When we taste it, we know it is the only right way.

We are holy because we believe and abide in Jesus, linked deeply into his holiness and living out of it. Being holy is not just about ourselves, our special private friendships, and our exquisite churches. Holy is heavenly, but also so earthy, and moves us into the world more deeply than ever. Holy can be when we welcome the refugee and make that classy chicken dish that has both mayonnaise and sour cream and place it in the middle of our tables and say, "Dig in!" to whomever drops by.

* * *

A little boy once gave Jesus fish and bread, his own food, and Jesus multiplied it to feed thousands. Hundreds of years later, we still tell this simple, beautiful story. It probably seemed like a little thing at first on that day when the boy wandered by with his lunch. We all live our own small stories, with no idea what the impact will be.

God is not tame. Jesus is not our pet. Our stories are not as boring as they might seem on some days. We are part of the big wild story of the restoration of heaven and earth, even on the Tuesdays when everything is going wrong.

We do not remain the same, not even the ministers' wives who can be so grouchy on the inside. And one of the wonderful things about being a minister's wife is that you hear stories of people dying to themselves and changing and doing hard but necessary things and realizing that God has been with them all along, every minute. They are less of a wreck than they used to be. I am less of a wreck than I used to be.

We are all still reluctant and peevish and afraid sometimes. I am. It has been easier for me to do things like travel to Cambodia and melt like wax in the hot sun building a water filter for schoolkids than to give money away, for example. Brent ushered tithing into our marriage, and for me it was like going to the gym—something I knew I needed to do and wanted to want to do, but it hurt.

I contemplated all the other things we could do with that money. I thought about new clothes and trips and ease and purple tulips for the living room whenever I saw them, and yes, skin serums in glass bottles that plump and nourish and fill in and stave off. I thought about not worrying and living without a mortgage and eating more of the world's best egg rolls from the Golden Palace just down the road.

I have grown in grace enough to know that it is okay to think of those things, but I must not surrender to my thoughts for long. So unruly me clings to discipline. Pre-authorized giving helps with my sanctification. It is a discipline to do good and give well. I don't always want to—my heart hesitates. I assume this is why there are commandments. Sometimes living out holy lives can take work—and a will. Holy living would be easier in a convent, I assume, and Brent could just visit. And he could tell people his wife is a nun, instead of me telling people my husband is a priest.

I need people to require hard things of me so that I will do the things that are hard.

The discipline of tithing and other charitable chores gradually, over years, loosens my tight grip on all I own, all my treasure, and forces all of that off to the side, not lodged in my heart at the very center of who I am. The continual year-after-yearness works in us to make all giving less uncomfortable and more of a holy pleasure—because, yes, we are growing plants, tended by a loving Master.

*   *   *

I cooked the capon I found at the Produce Depot around the corner for a dinner with Brian, the son of Sue and Ned, who were always kind to us back at our old church.

When we moved here, where their youngest son lived, we wanted to reach out and hug him into our lives a bit. So I bought the extra-large chicken to roast, and I was happy to think about the leftovers coming our way.

After dinner, Brian visited with Thomas in front of that giant TV in the next room. Brent wrapped up all the leftover meat to send home with Brian. He created a package of tin-foil almost a foot high—that's how much was left.

I was a little surprised. "Does he need that much?" I asked.

Brent answered, "He can make sandwiches, a single guy like that."

I shushed him. He was too loud, and I didn't want Brian to hear—to think I would ask such a thing or care that Brent was giving away all the leftovers.

"Do you have bread at home, Brian?" Brent called out.

He was going to give Brian our bread too.

Brent left the kitchen. I was alone with the chicken again. I could ease open the package and grab an inch or two of meat for lunch tomorrow.

I pictured myself committing this crime. Then I imagined them walking in on me as I rewrapped the leftovers, the foil crinkling like an alarm. I suppose I'd die. Even if I didn't get caught in the act of stealing back my own chicken, I'd have to explain to Brent where the leftovers had come from—that I had robbed the young bachelor who had just told us that on weekends he ate only McDonald's.

So I sat alone at the table, flipping through the newspaper.

"Do you need anything while I'm out?" Brent called as he walked out the door to drive Brian home.

I do.

I need a bigger, better heart. Mine was annoyed and closed down, doors tightly shut.

Royal priesthood of believers all the time, wretch sometimes. Holy, yes, but not wholly, yet.

The path through this, though, is clear and well marked and always open.

If someone asks for the chicken, say, "Here, take my bread too."

* * *

On my trip to refugee camps in South Sudan, I traveled with a radio reporter and a camera guy from a TV station, along with the organizer of the trip. He was from a charity that wanted to show the world their work and what was happening in South Sudan. He and I were the Christians on the team.

He asked the other two journalists about their relationship with the Lord. I cringed. I wondered if my cringe showed. I felt guilty for being embarrassed by the vigor of his witness. I really liked him, but we were crammed into a tiny plane flying north from Juba, the capital city, facing each other on small cracked seats. I wanted Tina, the cool radio woman, to like me—which is a trap left over from my childhood.

No one answered that, yes, they had a relationship with the Lord. Neither appeared to be the least bit interested in one.

Usually the topic of religion comes up around me anyway, whether I raise it or not, because of the writing I do and the work Brent does. Sometimes people simply volunteer that they are not religious and that they swear and drink and are real reprobates, the likes of which, they say, I have never seen. They don't know I have rye-soaked roots. This exchange on the plane felt forced, though, as stiff as the hard vinyl chairs we sat on.

We landed on the long red-dirt strip at the camp, goats scattering off in every direction. I averted my eyes from the remains of a plane wreck shoved off to the side, like an old car in someone's yard.

We camped in large green canvas tents, stretched out on our cots, jumping at every bang and bump we heard. Insects buzzed and hummed through the night like an orchestra. Tina and I bonded. That's what happens when you stumble together toward the latrine through the thick darkness of the African night and stop to see the stars so low and full and astonishing you could reach up and pick them from the night sky like apples from a tree. We became friends.

The next day we toured the camp, wandering slowly down narrow dirt roads and through the remarkable, astonishing heat. There were churches there led by pastors who had fled their devastated villages along with everyone else. We were not there on a Sunday, so I couldn't attend. If the pastors were married, I guessed that their wives were especially central here as they stood beside their husbands, organizing simple Sunday schools and singing louder than anyone to keep the music and worship going. The service would have lasted for hours, or so I have heard. A long holiness. There is no place on this earth that does not have the potential to reveal the holy, and it might be especially visible in places of refuge.

We met Peter, a logistics coordinator helping to figure out food rations.

"God is here right now, working in this place with these people," Peter said. He seemed impossibly young to me to be doing such big and good things. Briefly I felt I had wasted my life.

"What better place to come and learn about God than where I think his heart is beating the most? For the marginalized and the poor," said Peter.

And then he added, "God is a mystery always unfolding."

The discomfort of talking boldly about God to my traveling companions melted like butter. *Look at those open hands and that open heart. Look at Jesus, right here in the refugee camp. Why wouldn't you want some of this in your life?*

I lived in this home called the church. I loved a man who was a priest. Peter and the people he worked with had given up something to be here. All the risk and unknown they had embraced because of their faith was part of being the church. They were the Church of Doing and Being Good. It just felt holy. And it was just as real as the Church of Tripping Over Its Own Feet and the Church of Saying Awkward Things.

Faith can curl up under covers and go to sleep like a cat if we let it. But then someone comes along and nudges it and says, "Wake up. There is beautiful work to do." And faith awakens. It stands and stretches. It is always better to be awake.

The church was there in that place, love made real, applying bandages and filling up water bottles. People did not think faith was crazy; they knew it was necessary. Even though Brent was not with me, I felt proud of my husband and his calling. We were part of this Big Church, this balm to the world and to every wound.

At night in our tent, I talked with Tina about my faith and how I came to be married to a minister. We warmed up to each other, sweltering on our cots. The hard edges there softened everything.

When I returned home and wrote my article, Peter remained on my mind. I looked up his home phone number and made a call. His mom answered, which is what I had hoped for.

"My name is Karen," I told her, "and I just came back from South Sudan. I met your son there." I told her how holy it all was, even though I did not use that word. Peter's mother started to cry.

"I never hear from that kid," she said. That's because Peter is a guy just like any other guy set apart by Christ, redeemed and holy, who still does not call his mother.

"You can be very proud of him," I said.

* * *

"That dog is so needy!" Brent would say in dismay as Dewey trotted from guest to guest whenever our living room was full.

"He's not needy," I would answer. "He's loving."

That's why I knew he'd be perfect as a therapy dog, if he could only pass the test, which included performing maneuvers of various kinds in front of a crowd of eager wannabes.

We were all there at 8:00 p.m., with our partners lying at our feet on six-foot-long leashes (flat collars only!). I had walked Dewey for three hours earlier that day. I was stiff but he was mellow, and that was my strategy since he barks at other dogs like a soldier at his post. I walked into this night thinking we'd likely fail these tricky tests.

He must have sensed what was at stake—old ladies cooing his name and, surprisingly, letting him lick their soft, powdered faces. I whipped him into a frenzy when I tossed a ball toward the middle of the room. I calmed him down quickly, as instructed.

An old man in a bathrobe moaned like a patient in pain. Dewey licked his hand and glanced around the room, bored. Then we had to cross paths with another owner and her dog, a black Lab that Dewey had been exchanging glances with since the session began.

"Stop and chat with each other," said the woman in charge of the evaluation. "Let's see how they interact." Would they show their teeth? Snarl? I assumed we were doomed, but when our dogs French-kissed, I knew we had passed.

When I first met her, Millicent, a minister's wife, was a hundred years old and lived in a small apartment in a seniors' home just down the street. She was number four on my list of seniors who wanted me to come by with Dewey for therapy-dog visits.

During our visits we moved from room to room, furnished with belongings edited and condensed and packed into these spaces with all that remains from eighty-plus years. South African art hung on Millicent's walls, a reminder of when she and her husband, long gone now, had lived and served at a church there so many years ago.

"What was it like to be a minister's wife back then?" I asked.

"I wasn't very good at it," Millicent said.

"Oh, I'm sure you were," I replied.

I was thinking that back then things were clear and well defined, with the roles spelled out for everyone, like a scripted play with stage directions. How could elegant and kind Millicent not have been good at it?

Of course, I know the feeling of not being good enough is real. Clearly it can last a lifetime.

"Before, John thought that you weren't a very good minister's wife, but now he thinks you are a good minister's wife," said a woman at church to me once.

She meant this as a gift, and so I accepted it as one.

"Oh, thank you," I said. But still I wondered, *What was I doing wrong before? What am I doing better now?*

Millicent told me she had once been in a church meeting with other ladies when a mouse dashed across the floor and perched for a second on her foot.

"I let it sit there," she said.

I wondered what the other ladies might have thought

about their minister's wife sitting in a meeting with a mouse on her foot, a tiny rebellion against expectation. For just a second, Millicent had departed from the script.

Gradually, as the weeks went on, I spent more time with Millicent than anyone. This was not good therapy-dog practice, but I liked her so much. I felt that magical minister's wife connection. I knew something crucial about her and her heart because she had served alongside her husband, supporting him, worshiping with him, helping him, listening to him preach week in and week out.

Maybe sometimes they had thought about a different life and then shook their heads clear of that. Maybe after reading the paper they had read *The Imitation of Christ* over their coffee in the morning, like Brent and I try to do before charging off in our different directions.

I thought of the years Millicent had spent serving with her husband, loving him through the light and the shadows that every ministry brings, and then of the years she had spent alone without him after he had died and gone on without her. I guessed it had gone by like a race for her, and now she lived in this quiet, small room, her big black Bible with its worn, softened cover on the table beside her.

I could end up like this, I thought. *And I would not mind.*

Dewey loved Millicent and ate the Kleenex from her crowded side table whenever he could. Finally the day came when I told her it was my last visit. We were moving to a new church in a city four hours away. I was sad to end my visits with Millicent, faithful and holy in her room after all these years and still wondering sometimes whether she had been a good enough minister's wife.

"You were, Millicent," I said. "I am sure of it."

"Thank you," she said.

"Millicent, I will see you again, on the other side," I told her. "Maybe there's a nice lounging area in heaven, just for ministers' wives."

We both laughed. She would be in heaven very soon, I was sure.

She looked up at me from her armchair, oxygen tank by her side. She wore a lovely pastel blouse and matching pants that her daughter had bought her, just a little bit dressy for a weekday, as befit her style.

"The Lord bless you and keep you," Millicent said as she raised her quavering hand with its fragile, parchment-like skin. She traced the sign of the cross through the air, and it hung there between us, a benediction in that tiny room.

"The Lord make his face to shine upon you and be gracious to you," she said. "The Lord lift up his countenance upon you and give you peace."

Millicent blessed me. I am blessed.

* * *

Last Christmas Eve we were late to church, as usual. I picked up Thomas after his shift at the drugstore, which ended after church had begun. On the way downtown, through the snowstorm to the service, he changed into "all the wrong clothes" I had brought from his closet.

Brent's visiting parents were already there, sitting with Holly. They had staked out a good spot down in the second row and on the right side—all the better to watch up close as their son preached. I would have had us farther back by at least ten rows, not quite so much in Brent's face and space. I'm not often a front-row minister's wife. I like to move around.

But when you have a good seat near the front, you can see all the saints, each and every one, passing by on their way to kneel at the front of the church and receive the bread and the wine, those symbols of the saving, broken body. We are a progression of the sick and the healed, the content and the conflicted.

There was Jessie and her son Max; Hazel and Bob, who make us the best Indian food ever; Kate, who runs the Friday night outreach; and Andy, who always asks Thomas about school and rugby. *Thank you.*

There was Christine, who had helped us with our garden when we moved. There was that couple whom Brent would marry soon, helping to usher them into the rest and hopefully the best of their lives. He is part of their story, and they are part of ours at least for a time, and yes, this is for better or for worse. Then I saw the woman who had shushed us, our entire family.

"Brent!" I had said after the shushing service, as he took

off his robes in his freezing-cold office. "A lady told us to be quiet."

"Well, you guys really can be loud," he answered. And that was the end of that.

But still there she is and here I am most every week, the church together.

There, in that line heading to Communion, were doubt and certainty, the rare and the ordinary, what can go wrong in a life in a moment and all that can go right, all beloved and restored and inching our way to heaven on our weak knees. We were there together. Broken, but being fixed. And I was part of this messy, beautiful grace, all of our stories unfolding in this home of rich and difficult blessings. I was right there in the middle of it.

EPILOGUE

"I LOVE YOU," Amara says after I slide into her pew near the front of the church. She touches the side of my face with her small hand. "Your hair looks funny."

She is my very young pal, the four-year-old daughter of Michele and Arnold. There is more silver in my hair now than when Amara first met me, and that is what catches her eye tonight. I've stopped coloring it; the bold truth of my hair surprises her.

I slide my backpack under the pew and catch my breath. I rushed here after an afternoon of shopping for a mother-of-the-groom dress that will not make me look like the mother of the groom. Some of the dresses designated "mother of the groom" are too sparkly for me. They seem to come with capes and require shoes beyond my abilities. Erik will marry

Nicoli soon, who, by a kindness I could not have imagined, is a minister's daughter. She understands.

Arnold is being ordained, and the special service is happening at our church. The bishop has asked our church to host and Brent to preach. Since family is far away and she might need a hand with the kids, Michele asked me to sit with her to help with Amara; Augustine, who is two; and Anselm, their new baby.

Amara and Augustine are puppies at our feet, scooting around the floor, bouncing up to look at the pews filling with parishioners from both rural churches Arnold has been called to serve. Then down they go again, spinning. Already they are very good at being minister's kids.

This old church looks beautiful tonight. The early evening light blurs a multitude of cracks in the plaster. The pews have been dusted with close attention for a service such as this.

A scarlet red vestment—a priestly garment—is hung over the back of the pew in front of us, arranged and ready for Michele's part in the service. Bishop Charlie asked her to help him place it on her husband after Arnold makes his vows. I am touched by this. It's a good idea.

"Watch those sticky fingers," Michele warns the kids, who are now inching closer to the vestment.

"Remember how great is this treasure committed to your charge," Bishop Charlie will read. "They are the sheep of Christ for whom he shed his blood. The Church and Congregation whom you will serve is his bride, his body."

The words are printed in the bulletin so we can all follow

along with the sacred vows and lifelong promises made by Arnold but accepted also by Michele and these sweet children. They sense something big is happening even though they are so little, spirits rising by the minute.

The congregation sings the opening hymn loudly. This is no funeral. Ordinations are joyful.

Arnold lies down face-first at the feet of the bishop, arms spread wide, cruciform on the floor of the hundred-year-old church: a show of submission that startles. I have never seen anyone do this. Arnold is a very tall man who played NCAA basketball for four years. His body stretches past our pew, like a fallen oak tree.

"Does Daddy have an owie?" whispers Augustine. I smile at hearing the word for a wound that my own children once used.

Not yet. But he will.

Church hurts. Church heals. They will need courage and warm, sturdy hearts.

Somewhere between "The Church's One Foundation" and the Nicene Creed, I move myself and the kids into the nursery with the bright murals painted on the wall and the second-hand dolls seated expectantly in their tiny high chairs. A wooden train set occupies Augustine almost immediately. Amara swings one of the dolls into a plastic stroller and mothers her for a while. And Anselm? He is full of despair. This appears to be the worst evening of his life. He weeps and wails in my arms. I dip and sway and swing, singing partial lullabies and verses from praise choruses. He is not falling for any of these half-baked moves.

That's okay. I get it.

I wonder where they are in the service. *Has Michele stood up yet and draped the red vestment on the man she has vowed to love in the office he has vowed to hold?*

Months from this night, I will make an emergency supper run to their house. In one of those strange mishaps on a staircase during a birthday party, Michele will be poked very hard in the eye by a tiny finger, and she will need a friend, or at least supper. She will need a minister's wife.

I will dash through the grocery store and grab things off shelves to make a spaghetti casserole and a salad. I will toss a small vanilla-bean cake (whatever that is) and two bags of animal crackers in the cart, one for the kids and one for the parents. Everyone I know eats their children's animal crackers behind their little backs.

I will reach for Anselm when we arrive at their house, the baby who has plumped up beautifully and will not appear to recognize me, unless he covers it up nicely. Anselm and I will look at each other, amused and reconciled like old friends. He will touch my arm so very lightly, reminding me of the chickadees that sometimes land on our hands in the park.

For now, though, we are here at the church on this ordination night. I am her helper, ineffective nanny, and new friend, holding and trying to comfort tiny, bereft Anselm. Then she appears, like a small miracle—the minister's wife, her face perfectly framed in the nursery window, here to soothe her child, tuck him in closely beside her heart, and head back into the church.

Acknowledgments

IF YOU'VE READ THIS FAR, you understand that being a minister's wife has not always been easy for me. The churches where Brent has served, with their warm and welcoming congregations, have made it easier. Thank you. I am grateful to the people in those places whose love has shaped me and whose faith has moved me. I really wasn't taking notes the whole time; I want you to know that. Thank you also to my parents, Russ and Marian Durling; my sister, Miriam Cleough; and my parents-in-law, David and Evelyn Stiller, for allowing me to write even a little bit about our shared stories and for always cheering me on.

When I decided to return to school in my middle years, I thought I was beefing up my credentials to teach writing, a new chapter of my vocation I had hoped to explore. Instead, I wrote a book about being a minister's wife. The master of fine arts in creative non-fiction from University of King's College in Halifax gave me a home for that. They embraced me and this project. I would never have written this book without them. Thank you to my mentors, Jane Silcott and Harry Thurston, and to my sisters in writing: Marsha, Robin, Alison, and Rebecca. What fun we had. Thank you to my agent, Hilary McMahon of Westwood Creative

Artists, for taking me on and believing in me and this book. When she called me to say she liked it, I jumped around my living room, like writers do.

When I first spoke to Sarah Atkinson, associate publisher at Tyndale House Publishers, I knew she "got" the book. When I first worked with editor Bonne Steffen, I knew it would be better under her watch. I felt protected and released at the same time, which I think, ideally, is how a writer of spiritual memoir should feel. Thank you. Every member of the Tyndale House team made me feel welcomed and supported, and I was impressed by their excellence. To the teams who worked on the book, from the copyediting to the cover and everything in between and after, thank you so much. I felt like I was part of a big family.

Thank you to the people whose stories I tell in this book, because their stories bumped up against mine and made an impact. Thank you for showing me something more about God and for allowing me to write about that. You led me deeper, and I am grateful.

During the writing of this book, I led a retreat for clergy wives in New Brunswick. I locked them in a room and read parts of my book out loud to them. Their reactions helped shape at least one chapter, especially when they didn't laugh at the funny bits but resonated with the painful parts. They encouraged me and gave me back my energy to keep writing and rewriting. Thank you, Clergy Spouses Retreat of the Anglican Diocese of Fredericton.

In the book I mention the special friendships that can rise up among ministers' wives. What a gift those friendships have been to me over the years. My Bible study group of ministers' wives in Ottawa is so awesome. If you are married to a pastor and don't have a group like that in your life, please start one.

Just as ministers' wives need other ministers' wives, writers need other writers. If you're a writer without a writing friend, find one. Thank you to Patricia Paddey, who rejoiced when I rejoiced all through this process.

Ministers' wives raise pastors' kids. I am so grateful to Erik, Holly, and Thomas for being my companions in the pew. You are so beautiful.

Brent did not read this book until I was about to sign on the dotted line. I have a courageous husband. His vocation made me a minister's wife, but it is his love that has helped me more closely become the woman I think God has called me to be. I know it has not always been easy. So thank you, finally and always, to the minister—my husband, Brent.

Notes

29   "Jesus said, 'Put your finger here,' and Thomas did believe . . ." See John 20:27.

29   "Jesus says that people should become like little children to enter the Kingdom of Heaven." See Matthew 18:1-4.

30   "The verse we were studying that day from 2 Peter touched on the matter of angels behaving badly." See 2 Peter 2:4.

33   "Holy, holy, holy! Lord God Almighty! Early in the morning our song shall rise to thee." *The Worshiping Church: A Hymnal* (Carol Stream, IL: Hope, 1990), 2.

CHAPTER 3—COMMUNITY

49   "'The first service that one owes to others in the fellowship consists in listening to them. Just as love to God begins with listening to His Word, so the beginning of love for the brethren is learning to listen to them.' . . . Bonhoeffer calls this the 'obligation of listening.'" See Dietrich Bonhoeffer, *Life Together* (New York: Harper & Row, 1954), 97–98.

54   "'The real sinew of community, the muscle of *koinonia* [fellowship], is not in how well we impress each other . . . but in how well we inconvenience ourselves for each other.' It isn't having that makes us rich, she says; 'it's giving. Give sacrificially, live richly.'" See Ann Voskamp, *The Broken Way: A Daring Path into the Abundant Life* (Grand Rapids, MI: Zondervan, 2016), 175.

55   "And now knowing what we know, we are responsible, for love's sake, for the people and places that are ours—if we have eyes to see." Steven Garber, *Visions of Vocation: Common Grace for the Common Good* (Downers Grove, IL: IVP Books, 2014), 111.

55   "'This is my body, broken for you.' He took a cup of wine, shared it,

and said that sipping from that goblet meant they were entering into a
new covenant with him and with each other." See Luke 22:19-20.

55   "The Bible also says that Jesus stripped down to the bare minimum,
wrapped a towel around his waist, got down on his knees, and did the
work of a servant, washing the feet of his disciples . . ." See John 13:3-17.

CHAPTER 6—FRIENDSHIP

108   "'Well done, sweet friend!' we can say to each other until we hear those
words much later, for the last and best time." See Matthew 25:23.

CHAPTER 7—FUNERALS

109–10 "Create and make in us new and contrite hearts, that we, worthily
lamenting our sins and acknowledging our wretchedness, may obtain
of you, the God of all mercy, perfect remission and forgiveness . . ."
*The Book of Common Prayer and Administration of the Sacraments with
Other Rites and Ceremonies of the Church according to the Use of the
Anglican Church in North America Together with the New Coverdale
Psalter* (Huntington Beach, CA: Anglican Liturgy Press, 2019), 544.

110   "Have mercy upon me, O God, in your great goodness; according to the
multitude of your mercies wipe away my offences. Wash me thoroughly
from my wickedness and cleanse me from my sin." As quoted in *The Book
of Common Prayer . . . with the New Coverdale Psalter*, Psalm 51:1-2, 546.

110   "Remember that you are dust, and to dust you shall return." *The Book
of Common Prayer . . . with the New Coverdale Psalter*, 545.

112   "Earth to earth, ashes to ashes, dust to dust; in sure and certain hope
of the resurrection to eternal life, through our Lord Jesus Christ; who
shall change our perishable body, that it may be like his own glorious
body, according to the mighty working of his Spirit, whereby he is able
to subdue all things to himself." *The Book of Common Prayer . . . with
the New Coverdale Psalter*, 261.

115   "I also know Jesus called what comes after this 'paradise' when he told
the thief on the cross beside him they'd be there together on that day, a
bit later in the afternoon." See Luke 23:32-43.

115   "I know there will be a new heaven and a new earth because that is
what the Bible says and what our faith teaches." See Isaiah 65:17,
66:22; 2 Peter 3:13; Revelation 21:1.

CHAPTER 8—ENVY

136   "I do remember that Jesus advises us to store up for ourselves treasures
in heaven, not on earth. I do know that my heart will follow my
treasure." See Matthew 6:19-21.

136   "I know Jesus said we cannot serve two masters. It is God or money." See Matthew 6:24.

136   "Even though it's uncomfortable, it is helpful to me that our faith requires us to not be so attached to stuff; that we are commanded not to covet, including our neighbor's donkey, if they have one." See Exodus 20:17.

136-7   "'Look at the birds of the air,' says our King Jesus. 'They do not sow or reap or store away in barns, and yet your heavenly Father feeds them.'" See Matthew 6:26.

CHAPTER 9—PRAYER

144   "cast all your anxiety on [God] because he cares for you." 1 Peter 5:7.

145   "'No, I'm not with him, not one of them,' he said to a girl who noticed him sitting by a fire in the courtyard." See Luke 22:54-60.

145   "Yet after his resurrection, Jesus came back and offered Peter a chance to say he was sorry—and Peter did, a few times in a few ways." See John 21:15-19.

146   "I cry out by day, but you do not answer, by night, but I find no rest." Psalm 22:2.

148   "His prayers include lines like 'Thank you, God, for giving us ordinary lives' and 'Weird Lord, you never promised us a rose garden, but right now we could use a few daisies or zinnias.' Hauerwas writes, 'God does not want us to come to the altar different from how we live the rest of our lives. Therefore I do not try to be pious or to use pious language in my prayers. I try to speak plainly, yet I hope with some eloquence, since nothing is more eloquent than simplicity.'" See Stanley Hauerwas, *Prayers Plainly Spoken* (Downers Grove, IL: IVP, 1999), 89, 84, 14.

153   "What do you want me to do for you?" Mark 10:51.

153   "until you have a prayer of about six to eight syllables that flows smoothly when spoken aloud and captures the core of your deep yearning for wholeness and well-being in Christ." Ruth Haley Barton, *Sacred Rhythms: Arranging Our Lives for Spiritual Transformation* (Downers Grove, IL: IVP, 2006), 76.

CHAPTER 11—FORGIVENESS

175   "He focused on Joseph, whose brothers had hated him, selling him into slavery because they were so jealous of him—and not just over the gorgeous coat he had, although that was part of it." See Genesis 37:1-36.

175   "Years later, Joseph saved them when famine struck their land and they

found themselves in his new homeland, hoping for a break. Joseph was their break." See Genesis 42:1-6.

175 "Later Joseph told his brothers that what they had meant for bad, God had meant for good." See Genesis 50:19-20.

178 "We confess that we have sinned against you in thought, word, and deed, by what we have done, and by what we have left undone. We have not loved you with our whole heart; we have not loved our neighbors as ourselves." *The Book of Common Prayer and Administration of the Sacraments with Other Rites and Ceremonies of the Church according to the Use of the Anglican Church in North America Together with the New Coverdale Psalter* (Huntington Beach, CA: Anglican Liturgy Press, 2019), 130.

CHAPTER 12—CHRISTMAS

189–90 "We shrank the number of gifts we bought for our children to three, modeling our giving after those wise men." See Matthew 2:11.

CHAPTER 14—HOLINESS

216 "He says that after a reordering of our relationship with God, 'reaching out to our fellow human beings' is the second kind of transformation we undergo in our spiritual lives. Nouwen described it as a movement 'from hostility to hospitality.'" See Henri Nouwen, *Reaching Out* (New York: Image Books, 1986), 63.

216 "Hospitality is 'one of the richest biblical terms that can deepen and broaden our insight in our relationships to our fellow human beings,' he wrote." See Nouwen, *Reaching Out*, 66.

218 "A little boy once gave Jesus fish and bread, his own food, and Jesus multiplied it to feed thousands." See John 6:1-15; see also Matthew 14:13-21; Mark 6:32-44; Luke 9:10-17.

222 "If someone asks for the chicken, say, 'Here, take my bread too.'" See Matthew 5:40.

229 "The Lord bless you and keep you . . ." See Numbers 6:24-26.

EPILOGUE

234 "Remember how great is this treasure committed to your charge. . . . They are the sheep of Christ for whom he shed his blood. The Church and Congregation whom you will serve is his bride, his body." Anglican Church in North America, "The Form and Manner of Ordaining a Priest," Episcopal Services/Ordination of a Priest, accessed November 21, 2019, http://bcp2019.anglicanchurch.net/index.php /downloads/.

About the Author

KAREN STILLER is a writer with more than twenty years of experience. She serves as a senior editor of the Canadian magazine *Faith Today* and hosts The Evangelical Fellowship of Canada's podcast. As a journalist, Karen has shared stories from South Sudan, Uganda, Senegal, Cambodia, and across North America. She moderates the Religion and Society Series at the University of Toronto, a debate between leading atheists and theologians. Her work has appeared in *Reader's Digest* and *The Walrus*, among other publications. Karen holds a master of fine arts in creative non-fiction from University of King's College, Halifax, and an honorary doctorate from Providence University College and Theological Seminary. She and her husband, Brent, a priest with the Anglican church, live in Ottawa, Canada, and have three adult children.

Have you visited
TyndaleChurchConnect.com
lately?
You'll find
• resources for your church;
• first chapters;
• discussion guides;
• author videos and book trailers;
• podcasts;
• and more!
Tyndale
CHURCHCONNECT
CP1546